HOW TO PLAN
A FUNERAL

HOW TO PLAN
A FUNERAL

And Other Things You Need to Know
When a Loved One Dies

LIZ COWEN FURMAN

BEACON HILL PRESS

OF KANSAS CITY

Library of Congress Cataloging-in-Publication Data

Furman, Liz Cowen.
   How to plan a funeral : and other things you need to know when a loved one dies / Liz Cowen Furman.
      p. cm.
   Includes bibliographical references.
   ISBN-13: 978-0-8341-2375-5 (pbk.)
   ISBN-10: 0-8341-2375-4 (pbk.)
   1. Death—Religious aspects—Christianity. 2. Funeral Rites and ceremonies. I. Title.
   BT825.F87 2008
   265'.85—dc22

                                                                          2008023997

10 9 8 7 6 5 4 3 2 1

To Rick,
who taught me to endure with grace.

⌒ CONTENTS

～ ACKNOWLEDGMENTS

A million thanks to Evergreen Memorial Park, Ron and Carol Lewis, and especially Cindy Peterson for helping me find the way while writing and researching this book and grieving the loss of Papa.

Thanks to Dave Furman and Jan Sperry for their expert editing and encouraging skills.

A special thank-you to Mark and Melissa Whaley, who let me stay in their home while they were away so I could have uninterrupted time to finish the book in the eleventh hour.

Blessings to Dana Oswalt for her encouragement and friendship. A true sister in the Lord.

** ** *

Many, many thanks to the scores of wonderful friends and family the Lord sent to help create this book. They shared ideas, edited my stuff, and prayed the book into existence. Their prayers, support, and belief in me are what brought this book into being.

Rod & Ronna Adams, Peggy Barkelew, Linda Berry, Dave Biebel, Neal & Peggy Browne, Carol Brumfield, Lynn Callison, Jim & Valerie Chapman, Linda Christianson, Bruce & Lisa Cole, Jim, Mary Ellen, & Alex Covino, Barbara Cowen, Glen & Dorothy Cowen, Paula Cowen & John Belfrage, Seth, Sean, & Brice, Bill & Debbie Cron, Dave & Verleen Didier, Erin, Josiah, & Alyssa Didier, Sue Doerner Ken & Jana Elliott, Eileen Fenner, Brad & Jane Cowen-Fletcher, Jo & Freeman Fletcher, Molly Frauenhoff, Barb Fredrickson, Sue Freytag, Dave Furman, Muff Furman, Martin Furman, Matthew Furman, Micah Furman,

Wayne & Jane Furman, Danny & Charlene Gevara, Alana Gevara, Aubree Gevara, Jacob Gevara, Joshua Gevara, Miriam Gevara, Cindy Giles, Melanie Green, Kathy Grossmann, Allyson Guy, Melany Hansen, Sabina Harte, Zahari Herbert, Tom & Peggy Hickman, Nikki Hooks, Peg Hooper, Heidi Hoskinson, Lisa Howell, Sandy Jackson, Jeremy & Charissa Jones, Maddie Jones, Rylie Kilgore, Phil & Joy Kinney, Pastor Keith & Lois Kraakevik, Catherine Kuck, Ron Lint, Kim McCallum, Don & Lorna McPeck, Jake & Emily Myers, Glen & Clara Mizenko, Nicholas & Rachel Mizenko, Kathy Moore, Josh, Brittney, & Keeley Myers, Jeff & Jennifer Myers, Deb O'Connell, Dana Oswalt, Bonnie Perry, Judi Perry, Cindy Peterson, Jed Rairdon, April Ringnalda, Mary Rouse, Jerry & Beth Schroppel, Eli & Jake Schroppel, Jan Scott, Theresa Sidebotham, Liz Siedenburg, Bruce & Teresa Simms, Dena Simonds, Tom, Cheryl, & Ian Smith, Olivia & Keith Soto, Sue Speight, Steve & Jan Sperry, Nika Star, Dick & Koann Stark, Joan & Bill Starnes, Jean Stewart, Tom, Kara, & Ben Stewart, Theresea Stimatze, Fred & April Struck, Michelle Sweeney, Bun & Cindy Tadlock, Kathy Taraba, Paul Thalos, Carrie Thomas, Leah Trisler, Elizabeth Turner, Glen & Christy Vandine, Jamie Verstreeter, Kurt & Lucia Von Fay, Ahna & Emilie Von Fay, Alyssa Wahr, Aletia Westlake, Mark & Melissa Whaley, Sid & Margie Whitfield, Sandy Wilkerson, Dick & Joy Wilsted, Mark & Kathy Wood, Phoebe & Woody Wood, Janice York, Tosha Zabka.

～ INTRODUCTION

Our whole family was coming to town in just two weeks to celebrate my father-in-law's 80th birthday. Mel, or Papa, as our boys called him, had terminal cancer, and death was imminent. However, it would come sooner than we expected.

We took Mel to see the oncologist on Friday because of some shortness of breath he was experiencing. The doctor decided to admit him for tests. I sat in the waiting room with my mother-in-law, Muff; my husband, Dave; my sister-in-law, April; and her husband, Fred. While we waited, we discussed Mel's upcoming birthday celebration.

Unexpectedly, a nurse approached us and told us that if we wanted to say good-bye to Mel, we should come with her. Good-bye? We were stunned.

Our three sons were 45 minutes away. My brother-in-law and sister-in-law were in a plane somewhere over Kansas.

We filed silently into Mel's room. His blood pressure was very low. We stood around his bed shouting our good-byes, as he was hard-of-hearing. We told him we loved him, and we thanked him for being a good dad, husband, and friend.

Muff spoke right into his ear: "Save a space for me."

April said, "Jesus is waiting for you, Dad."

Mel looked at each of us and then focused on Dave. He whispered, "Take care of Mom." Then he looked at Muff, his wife of nearly 60 years, and spoke in a soft voice that was barely audible, "I love you." A tear rolled down his cheek as the monitor flat-lined.

It was over.

We were directed to a small conference room nearby to compose ourselves. Mel's oncologist, who had been with us at the bedside, came in and said he hoped when he died that his family would be with him to share the same loving messages we had given Mel. If there's such a thing as a good send-off, Mel had it.

We sat for quite a while, not really knowing what to do. None of us had ever experienced anything like this, and we weren't sure what the appropriate next move should be. We made a few calls and then sheepishly asked a very compassionate nurse what we were supposed to do. She gave us a list of local mortuaries and asked us if we wanted to see Mel's body before they took him downstairs. We did not. Later, we all regretted that we did not remove his wedding ring for Muff.

My stomach was in knots as I drove to collect our three children, knowing I would have to share with them that their Papa had died. They had been expecting him to be released from the hospital the next day. They took it very hard and were terribly upset that they didn't get to say good-bye.

That evening we sat around as if in shock. The weight of the loss felt heavy on our chests—as if the wind had been knocked out of us.

The next morning I sent the boys out to play. Children have such a naturally healthful way of coping. They needed something to do. It didn't remove the pain, but as they focused on something else, it made it easier for them to talk about their loss.

We chose a wonderful memorial park from the list we had been given, one that was close by. I called and made an appointment to go in and make the arrangements.

I understand now what people mean when they say there's

no way we can ever be fully ready for a death. Even if it's expected, it inevitably comes as a shock. There's just no way you can totally prepare for it, emotionally or otherwise.

Dave pointed out that death is not how things were supposed to happen—we were created to live forever with the Father and Son, so death feels unnatural and awful to those of us left behind. In time, I realized the pain wouldn't kill me, though it seemed for a while that it might.

I'm now able to rejoice that I knew Mel. Knowing him and sharing life with him was well worth the pain of losing him.

When Mel died, it was the first time I was responsible for planning a loved one's celebration of life. I had no idea where to begin, and I couldn't find a book about it at the local bookstore.

As I write this book, I'm aware that you have likely just experienced the death of someone you love. Let me first say that I'm so sorry for your loss. Times of loss have, in my experience, been some of the greatest tests of my faith.

My prayer for you is that the Holy Spirit will give you peace that passes understanding as you journey down this dark road. Remember: whatever you're feeling is OK. Nothing surprises God. No expression of pain, anger, or despair we can muster is too big for Him to handle. You can be honest with Him; tell Him how you feel.

I encourage you to not let any person tell you how you *should* feel. Neither will it be helpful for you to expect your loved ones to react in a certain way. Be patient with yourself and with others. Take time to process the pain, and don't rush the process.

I hope this book will help ease the stress of making the many decisions you'll face, and may you find beauty from the ashes of your loss.

In His peace,

Liz Cowen furman

> *Come to Me, all who are weary and heavy-laden,*
> *and I will give you rest.*
> —Matt. 11:28, NASB

1 ～ CELEBRATING THE LIFE OF YOUR LOVED ONE
Planning the Funeral or Memorial Service

As you plan a funeral or memorial service for your loved one, here are some differences between the two.

A funeral is usually held soon after the person's death, and the body or cremated remains—usually referred to as "cremains"—will be present during the service. Usually a graveside service will immediately follow if the person's body is present.

A memorial service can be held at any time following the death, and the body is usually not present. I've heard of memorial or tribute services being held in advance of the death while the person is still alive and can attend, but that isn't customary.

Of the services I've attended, by far the most moving ones were the services that had a personal touch. Photographs, slides, collages, anything that helps tell the story of the loved one's life are appropriate and can be very touching.

I've always said that when my time comes, I hope the wake is more like a party. Nothing sad or mournful for me, thank you. I want the music, the room set-up, and even the lighting to set a festive mood. I like to think that there'll be plenty of great food, some wonderful music, and lots of photographs please. I'm looking forward to going to heaven, so I don't want a roomful of people crying for me.

When my father-in-law died, our goal was to make his service a celebration of his life. We wanted to highlight the high points of his life and share with folks who might not have known him as well as we did what a great guy he was.

I heard author Angie Hunt say recently that whether we admit it or not, we all want to have a great memorial service. Not flashy or expensive maybe, but we all long to leave a legacy, and we want our loved ones to express that our life mattered and that we'll be missed. She said that's why people carve their initials in trees and press their hands into concrete. It's because we want our lives to have counted for something.

A memorial service or funeral is the way we honor the memory of a person who has gone home. A well-planned service is, for many of those left behind, the beginning of the grieving process.

As you begin to plan the service for your loved one, include memories of him or her that will strike a chord with those who attend. A great deal of comfort can be gained from remembering the familiar and loved characteristics of the person. Also, funny stories seem to take the edge off the pain. When everyone is feeling sad and tearful, a good laugh brought about by a favorite memory or photograph helps.

At the service for our friend Linda, an open microphone was available for people to share their memories of her. At first, everyone who spoke talked about what a great encourager she was and espoused her great ability to see into someone's soul and find the good in that person. The tributes went on and on; they were very touching, and we were all bawling like babies. Then her husband got up and told a funny story about Linda, so other loved ones chimed in. They had everyone laughing and crying at the same time. It was a wonderful time of sharing and tribute.

I want to share with you ideas that others and I have used to plan a meaningful service. You may want to use them, or they may spur ideas of your own that you want to use. Ask others for their ideas; it's comforting to people to feel that they're part of the process. Delegate jobs to others so they can feel involved and included. Their involvement can be a powerful help in their healing process. Be careful to ask them to take part and not tell them what you expect them to do. If some prefer to not be involved, respect that.

If you would like to involve children in planning the service or even taking part in the service, it's certainly appropriate. Here are some ideas for ways to involve them.

Allowing Children to Participate in the Service

- Have children or grandchildren of the deceased carry to the front an item that represents something important to the one who has passed away.

    At a funeral my friend attended, one child carried a bag of potatoes, because his dad was famous for his potato recipe. Another carried a pair of snow skis, because his dad was an avid skier. Another brought forward a soccer ball, because his dad loved watching his son's soccer team play. As the items were brought to the front, the pastor told what it was and why it was important to this young father. The children felt very included without having to speak in front of those gathered for the service, and each child was allowed to choose what to carry forward.

- Don't rule out allowing youngsters to speak during the service.

    My son, then 14, wrote a eulogy for his Papa and delivered it with complete composure, and it was his idea to do it. We were surprised. I've since been to several funerals in which children got up and spoke. The key is to let them choose what's right for them. Don't apply pressure, give hidden messages, or goad them, regardless of how great you think it would be for them to take part in the service. Allow them to back out, even at the last minute, if they have a change of heart.

- If they play an instrument, let them.
- Ask them to hand out the order of service and obituary.
- Let them help with the set-up at the front of the sanctuary, deciding where flowers should be set or where pictures of the deceased or things he or she loved should be displayed.
- Let them help choose photos for the slide show or memory board.
- Let the children or grandchildren sing a song together if they would like to, but don't force them to take part.
- Ask them to hand out small bottles of bubbles to blow at the grave site or balloons to release after the service.
- Give them the opportunity to read scripture during the service.
- Invite them to do a reading, write a poem of their own to read, or print it and hand it out before the service.
- Take part in the "memory tree."

    For their 10-year-old daughter's funeral, one family had a "memory tree." Ribbons were handed out at the church door. People were invited to write memories on the ribbons and tie them to the branches. Later the family planted the tree at a park they had enjoyed visiting when their daughter was alive. Let the children pass out the ribbons and pens or tie the ribbons onto the tree.

- Take part in a "chocolate factory."

    To celebrate her husband's passion for all things choco-

late, Elaine and her children threw a chocolate dessert party after the funeral in the parking lot of a chocolate factory. There are many possible variations on this one that a family could do to tailor it to their loved one's passion.

- Ask children for their ideas about the music.
- Ask them if they have their own ideas about something special they could do.
- Let them help choose the gravestone, the casket, the urn, the flowers, or the vault if their age allows. Narrow their choices to items that are within your price range so they won't be disappointed by choosing something that can't be considered.

May the God of hope fill you with all joy and peace as you trust in Him, so that you may overflow with hope by the power of the Holy Spirit.

—Rom. 15:13

It may not seem like it now, but you'll get through this time. One thing that helped me so much was the assurance that we would survive, coming from people I love. Even though I wasn't convinced they were right at the time, it still was a comfort to me.

When I was 18 weeks along in my pregnancy, I suffered a miscarriage. I believed I caused it by taking a certain medicine. Although I had called the doctor's office and asked before taking the medication, I later learned that it could have caused the miscarriage. I was destroyed. It seemed too early in the pregnancy to have a memorial service, and some people told me that because it was so early it wasn't a real loss. But we longed to do something to show that this little life mattered and was very real to us. In the words of Dr. Seuss, "A person's a person no matter how small." A memorial service is an important step on the road of healing.

The word "funeral" sounds like such a dirge. Some people we know referred to their loved one's service as his "commissioning service." Other friends held a "graduation ceremony" to celebrate their loved one's graduation into heaven.

When Mrs. Drake, my son Martin's teacher, died, her family held a "life celebration." It was beautiful. Flowers and balloons were everywhere, and a big-screen photo show was conducted, accompanied by uplifting music and people sharing how her life had touched theirs. I remember thinking that I hoped they had taped the service so the family could watch it in the months to come and be encouraged.

At a funeral I recently attended there was a basket filled with small packages of tissues for whoever wanted one. It was a nice touch. I didn't think I would need any and didn't take a package. Later I was sorry I hadn't, so I think it would be a good idea to leave the baskets scattered throughout the pews.

A Sample Order of Service

Following is a sample for you to use as you plan the order of the service. Use what works for you, and discard the rest, or feel free to add your own touches. This outline is a good place to start without having to reinvent the wheel.

Order of Service
Prelude (Music)
Presentation of Colors
Greetings and Opening Remarks
Congregational Singing
Prayer
Song
Eulogy
Song

Open Microphone
Congregational Singing
Homily (Message)
Song or Congregational Singing
Prayer (Perhaps the Lord's Prayer)
Presentation of Flag and/or Taps
Retrieval of Colors
Postlude (Music)

The Music

Music is a powerful healer, and most services start with and end with music. Well written and well performed music can bring us to tears and can also lift us up. For the service, include a few of the songs your person loved, and include a few that will inspire and encourage. Music can also make a powerful faith statement, so be sure to include spiritual songs.

For my father-in-law's service we chose songs he and my mother-in-law loved. We set his slide show to those songs. The opening childhood and college pictures were set to Glenn Miller's "String of Pearls." For the family photographs we played Steve Green's "Find Us Faithful." The last photo was a recent close-up of Mel that we left up while "I Can Only Imagine" by MercyMe was played. Many people record the services now so that those who are too young to remember or unable to attend will feel included.

Our youngest son, Micah, who was nine years old, played "Amazing Grace" on the recorder. To close the service, Martin and Matthew, our two oldest sons, played "Taps" on their trumpets from the balcony. It was very touching and powerful.

Using carefully chosen songs adds a lot to the service. Be careful when asking someone to sing or play; live music can be a great addition or, when not done well, can derail an otherwise well-planned service. We played instrumental versions of favorite old hymns on a CD player as folks came in. Music has a way of ministering to broken hearts in ways words can't penetrate.

If you know an accomplished pianist, it's a wonderful touch to include live music. Live harp music or bagpipes also add beautifully to the service. Finding someone to play is a job that's good to delegate to someone you trust who wants to help. Remember—including others in the planning and execution of the service is a great way to make them feel a part of their loved one's last "party" and also helps that person start his or her healing as well.

The following is a list of songs my friend Lisa Cole of Promise Band and many other friends recommended. I've also given the names of the artists who recorded the songs. I hope this list helps you find something just right for the service you're planning.

"Abide with Me," Judy Collins or Tennessee Ernie Ford

"Amazing Grace," Charlotte Church or an instrumental version

"Angels Among Us," Alabama

"Ave Maria," Michael Bolton

"Baby, Take Your Bow," Chris Rice

"Back in His Arms Again," Mark Schultz

"Be Not Afraid," David Phillips

"Because He Lives," Bill and Gloria Gaither

"Because You Loved Me," Celine Dion

"Beyond Belief," Petra

"Blessed Assurance," Brian Free and the Assurance

"Breakfast Table," Chris Rice

"Bridge over Troubled Waters," Simon & Garfunkel

"Come, Now Is the Time to Worship," Phillips, Craig, and Dean

"Cry Out to Jesus," Third Day

"Draw Me Close," Lyndsey Wallace

"The Dance," Garth Brooks

"El Shaddai," Michael Card or John Thompson or Amy Grant

"Find Us Faithful," Steve Green

"Forever Is a Long, Long Time," Orquestra Was

"Friends," Michael W. Smith

"Give Me Jesus," Fernando Ortega

"Go Rest High on the Mountain," Charlotte Ritchie

"Going Home," Wayne Watson or Sara Groves

"Good-bye, My Friend," Linda Ronstadt

"He's Listening," Flo Price

"Home," Sara Groves

"Home Free," Wayne Watson

"How Great Thou Art," Daywind Performance Track

"How to Say Good-bye," Michael W. Smith or Amy Grant

"I Cannot Hide from God," Ralph Carmichael

"I Can Only Imagine," MercyMe

"I Miss My Friend," Daryl Worley

"I Surrender All," Amy Grant

"I Will Lift My Eyes," Bebo Norman Worship Tracks

"I Will Remember You," Amy Grant

"I Will Rest in You," Jaci Velasquez

"I Will Trust You, Lord," Sheryl Farris

"I've Just Seen Jesus," Larnelle Harris & Sandi Patty

"In Christ Alone," Margaret Becker

"In This Very Room," Sandi Patty

"It Is Well with My Soul," Greater Vision

"Jesus Will Still Be There," Point of Grace

"Lay It Down," Jaci Velasquez

"Legacy," Nicole Nordeman

"Lift My Eyes," Jill Paquette

"Lord's Prayer," Charlotte Church

"Mansion over the Hilltop," Daywind Performance Track

"May It Be," Enya

"My Tribute," André Crouch

"Near the Cross," Joel Rosenberger on piano

"On Eagle's Wings," Michael Crawford

"Psalm 23," Charlotte Church

"Praise You in This Storm," Casting Crowns

"Roses Will Bloom Again," Jeff and Sheri Easter

"Shout to the Lord," Integrity or LordSong

"The Lord's Prayer," Charlotte Church

"The Savior is Waiting," Ralph Carmichael

"The Old Rugged Cross," Vince Gill or Anne Murray

"'Tis So Sweet to Trust in Jesus," Amy Grant

"Trust His Heart," Wayne Watson or Babbie Mason

"What a Friend We Have in Jesus," Alan Jackson

"When the Savior Wipes the Tears from Our Eyes," The Hoskins
   Family

"Word of God, Speak," MercyMe

Collections of Songs:

50 Hymns on Guitar, Samuel David Erwin

Big Band Hymns, The Chris McDonald Orchestra

Celtic Hymns, Don Hart, instrumental

Hymns of Hope, David Davidson on violin

Lord of the Hymn, Celtic Worship

Praise Him Piano, CN Productions

Top 25 Praise Songs, 2005 Edition

When We All Get to Heaven, Echoes in the Valley, banjo and
   chimes

Consider any songs your loved one enjoyed that you feel would be appropriate. If there are favorites the congregation could sing along with, remember that singing is very healing. Be sure to project the lyrics onto a screen at the front or print them in the order of service.

At my friend Linda's service, her grandchildren sang "Jesus Loves Me" together. There is safety in numbers, and it was a way for all the grandchildren to participate. Remember: participation is up to the children, not a requirement.

Many of the songs listed here can be found on YouTube if you want to hear them. Some of the artists have clips on their Web sites, or you can listen to them at Christian bookstores where there are usually booths for listening to demo CDs.

The Order of Service or Memorial Folder

The order of service or memorial folder is usually handed out at the door as people come to the service. It usually includes the order of the service and information about the deceased. Often a photo is included. Sometimes a eulogy or the obituary that appeared in the newspaper along with poetry or a favorite Bible verse are included.

My father-in-law's sister writes poetry, and she wrote a wonderful personalized poem when Mel died. We had it copied onto beautiful paper and put one in each of the folders that were handed out. Many of the services I've attended included some poetry.

Sharing Time

Setting aside a portion of the service to allow friends and family members of the deceased to share memories of the person or talk about his or her character traits is often done. If you decide to include this in the service, make it optional. Ask those attending to share a favorite memory or something about the person they loved and will miss. It might be good to ask someone to share that you feel will be comfortable doing so to get things started. Be sure the pastor or the one conducting the service doesn't allow sharing to go on for too long.

If you don't feel comfortable with a time of sharing, another idea to give people an opportunity to reflect on the one who has died is to pass a binder with lined paper and a pen throughout the gathering. In one service I attended, pretty stationery sheets were passed around, and at another a journal-type book was passed around. Let folks tell their favorite stories or something that was meaningful to them about your loved one. Another idea is to put a sheet of paper and a self-addressed envelope in the folder so that folks can think about it and mail it later. These thoughts and remembrances make a great keepsake and source of comfort for the family.

Using Original Art in the Service

If your loved one was an artist or had a favorite artist, using one of his or her favorite pieces in the order of service, on a stand at the front or back of the room, or in the entry next to the guest book is very appropriate. I attended a service in which a color copy of a painting by the deceased was on the front of the order of service. Remember: anything your person created could be displayed on the table. Think outside the box. Quilts, sculptures, pictures of Christmas decorations, carved pieces, paintings, or knitting—anything he or she loved to make— would be a great tribute to the loved one's legacy.

Something He or She Loved

When my friend's mother-in-law passed away, the family asked everyone to come to the funeral in Bronco or Rockies attire because she was such a fan, and she hated to dress up. A fitting tribute!

At our friend Paul's funeral, there was a fly-by at the end of the service by Air Life. It was awesome. It gave folks the feeling that Paul was waving at everyone from heaven. A definite way to end on an up-note!

A Keepsake

At Robin Ann's memorial service there was a basket at the back of the church with little cards stapled to packets of flower seeds. The cards were about the size of a business card and read, "In loving memory of Robin Ann, August 14, 1958—May 7, 2007. Robin loved life and lived it to the fullest. In her honor, please carry on by planting these seeds." A nice touch.

Picture Displays

Foam core display board of a life well lived. I made one of these for Mel's service. We displayed it on an easel in the front of the room where the service was held. Mel was cremated, so we didn't have a coffin at the front. We filled the room with photos and other things he loved.

I went to the hobby store and purchased items I could use to make a board with his name, photograph, and favorite verse on it. I purchased big 3-D letters. I bought a foam core display board so it could stand on its own. They come in many colors, but can also be covered with beautiful fine art paper that comes in big sheets available at art supply or hobby stores. Because of the explosion of the scrap-booking industry, there are many great sticker choices. A few well-placed ones can add a lot. Beautiful paper to mount the picture and print a verse and text on comes for a few cents per sheet. I used a glue gun to attach the plastic letters and a scrap-booking glue stick with super holding power. I attached little metal shapes I found that depicted things Mel loved, such as traveling and the American flag. For the photographs, use repositionable tape to make them easier to remove later.

Photo albums. I've been to several services where the families brought in photo albums that were already completed. They were open on a table so that folks could take a few minutes to look through them and remember the good times. After the service, they were moved to the reception room so folks could linger over the pictures.

A time line. Another idea is to take several of the foam core poster boards and put photos in chronological order to make a timeline of the person's life. Or you can also group photos together in different activities the person enjoyed such as sports, gardening, cooking, and so on. These collages can be placed at the front of the room and then moved later to the reception room.

This works if you have many photos or if you have only a few. Be sure to attach the photos in a temporary way so they may be easily removed later. Again, stickers are available now for almost any occasion and will add a lot to the display.

A memory line. An easier idea for a photo display is to first collect as many photos as you would like to display. Print the photos and mount them on pretty paper. After putting them into chronological order, attach string to the wall by placing tacks on both ends and in the middle. Add a bow over each of the tacks. Next attach the photos to the string with clips or clothes pins. It makes a lovely memory line, and the photos can be easily removed to put in a photo album. A memory line is a great conversation-starter and gets everyone talking about the fun memories. My friend told me about a service she attended where memory lines were strung all around the room with many copies of each of the photos. After the service, every guest was encouraged to choose a picture he or she liked and take it home. People were very pleased to have a keepsake.

Centerpieces. Another way to honor the memory of the deceased is to put photos of him or her doing something he or she loved and grouping them for centerpieces for the tables. Photos of the person gardening, gathered around a pot of flowers, or photos of the person mountain biking, gathered around his or her helmet, make great centerpieces. Again, think outside the box.

Snapping plenty of pictures has taken on new meaning to me lately. I want to have photos of the folks I love so that I can represent them well if they go to heaven before me. Besides, I cherish looking at them and reliving all those precious memories.

A picture show. We wanted to honor Mel's great life, so we filled the room with reminders of him. I collected as many pictures as I could of my own and from other family members. Mel and Muff had celebrated their 50th wedding anniversary seven years before his death, and we made a book to commemorate the occasion; there were lots of photos close at hand. I took the entire pile to the copy shop and scanned them onto disks. You can do this at home if you have a scanner, but if not, you can scan them at a copy shop or a self-serve photo shop. Appropriate stickers add a lot, and there are many to choose from at your local hobby shop. I found some amazingly appropriate ones and scanned them and added music to make a wonderful Power-Point presentation.

If you're good with a computer, this is a snap. If you're computer-challenged, you can still do it. Ask for help—someone will be delighted to pitch in. Ask a kid—kids tend to know more about computers than adults. Remember: any way you can involve others in the process is good for them and reduces your stress.

A looping slide show. My friend Jean put together a slide show that was played in the entrance and then the reception room with accompanying background music. It was lovely, and since I hadn't known Jean's mother except in her later years, it was meaningful to see shots of her when she was young. Jean said a benefit to putting it together was that it was good therapy for the whole family to reflect on their loved one's life as they chose the photos together and relived precious memories.

There are also digital picture frames available now that play 2,000 digital photos like a slide show, and you can even add music. This is a great idea for funerals, but also a wonderful gift idea for aging parents. Wouldn't it be meaningful if the person who passed away was able to enjoy the slide show while he or she was alive?

Honoring the dead and respecting the living. As we prepared for Mel's service, I asked other family members what songs, photographs, or other items they thought characterized his life. I added every one of their suggestions if at all possible. Remember: a memorial service or funeral is really for those left behind, so cater to their needs and desires, and be respectful of their ideas of grief expressions—even non-expressions. Everyone deals with loss and pain in a personal way, so it's important to not impose our ideas on what's the proper way for someone else to grieve.

We encouraged my mother-in-law to bring her dog—a sheltie named Annie—to the service for support. As we expected, Annie was a great comfort to her, and she behaved perfectly during the service. I realize not all churches or funeral homes allow animals other than service dogs.

Do whatever feels comfortable and right for you and your loved ones. Don't worry about what anyone else thinks. At these times, it's important to seek as much comfort as possible for those who are hurting and not worry about doing anything to impress others.

Food for Thought: Refreshments Following the Service

Sometimes I think our culture has things a bit backwards. At weddings, the bride and groom—who are young and just starting out—have to come up with dinner for every guest who graces them with their presence. At funerals, we seem to expect the family—who is grieving and in agony—to throw a party. The Body of Christ is at its best during these times when there's a special need. We're directed by God's Word to stay in the fellowship of believers, because a burden shared is halved, and a joy shared is doubled.

If your church offers to help, let them. If you're able and want to thank them, make an offering to the group that supplies food for funerals, or write them a thank-you note—you can do that later. Now is the time to let the body work for you.

After the service, we offered coffee and dessert. My Bible study buddies and friends all brought food in, and they even served it and made the coffee. They're saints—every one. We didn't want to have a full-blown dinner; my mother-in-law wasn't up to sitting and making small talk. She was in pain. After other services I've attended, church members had laid a beautiful dinner table of food. Do whatever works for you. I never feel much like eating at such times, but many folks find it comforting, largely because of the fellowship that comes with a meal. Plus, remember that the out-of-towners have no place to go.

If you find yourself in the crisis of losing someone, as we did, and you're between churches, as we were because of a recent move, then here are some low-, medium-, and a little higher-budget ideas for refreshments after the service.

Low-Budget

- Don't schedule the service at meal time.
- Fruit—order trays or cut it up yourself.
- Cookies or pie—wholesale clubs have a wide selection at reasonable prices.
- Coffee, tea, water, and lemonade.

Medium-Budget

To the above add:

- Sandwich trays from the grocery or deli.
- Rolls & condiments.
- A relish tray or two—or pick up some jars of pickles.

  The store or restaurant that prepares the trays will be able to tell you how many each tray will serve. Estimating how many are coming to a funeral is difficult. If possible, err on the side of too much food, but try to purchase items that you can freeze or that will keep for several days. No one is likely to feel like cooking for a while—and may not even feel like eating, but, of course, everyone must eat, and it's good to have the leftover sandwich trays on hand.

A Little More Money with a Little Less Effort

If you can afford it, contact a favorite restaurant and have a light meal catered that can be served through a buffet line. Be

careful to not choose very aromatic foods, as some will sur[e] feeling queasy from the day's events and grief. Maybe p[i] restaurant that your person loved. For me, they can get f[r] from The Olive Garden. And don't forget the tiramisu a[nd] chocolate!

Again, be sure to choose things that can be used for sever[al] days that will make good leftovers or can be frozen. If you can afford it, this is a good option, and restaurant employees will come in and do the set-up and clean-up.

If you don't feel up to planning or serving food, just have coffee and tea and punch, and call it good. Be sure to listen to yourself and your limits. If you're stricken with heartache, couldn't care less about refreshments, and there's no help, don't even do it. No one with a brain will care, and if they do care, they should have been helping make it happen. This isn't about impressing anyone. It's about surviving a hard time.

If you want to serve food following the service, this is the perfect place to delegate! The work is easy, and it will give others something to do besides sit and cry.

Lord, as we contemplate the tribute to our loved one, please bring to mind the attributes that will encourage those left here and serve to extend our loved one's legacy. Show us what you would have us share, and give us your words. In Jesus' name we pray. Amen.

2 ～ CHOICES AND COSTS

So we are always confident, knowing that while we
are at home in the body we are absent from the Lord.
For we walk by faith, not by sight.
—2 Cor. 5:6-7, NKJV

When one we love dies, even if we were aware of a terminal condition, there is still a sense of being caught off-guard. How do we proceed? What is appropriate? What is meaningful? What arrangements should be made for the body our loved one inhabited?

It is common to feel overwhelmed. It is, after all, a big responsibility to make these important decisions and plan the service and burial or cremation of another. When you go to the funeral home to make the final arrangements, bring along a trusted friend or family member and ask him or her for input into the discussions and decisions.

Many recommend that the family should get three price quotes to avoid getting financially gouged during this vulnerable time. However, folks who have just lost someone can barely face one funeral director, much less three.

If you feel that way too, there are two questions to ask the funeral director when you make the initial call. Based on the answers, you will have an indication of whether or not you would like to proceed with that particular funeral home. By asking these questions you will be able to tell if he or she is amicable to whatever you would like for your loved one's service. Ask:

- What is the price for immediate—or direct—cremation?
- What is the price of the least expensive casket you offer?

If they won't give you a straight answer, call somewhere else. Look in the obituary section of your newspaper; if you notice that one funeral home seems to be getting the most business, there's probably a good reason. You can ask your pastor if he or she has a recommendation based on prior dealings with different funeral homes. Look in the advertising section of the phone book to see the services provided by each funeral home. Word of mouth is also a good way to learn about the funeral homes in your area. Regardless of whether you're seeking to have a traditional service or a not-so-traditional service or whether you are seeking to bury your loved one's remains or intend to have your loved one cremated, you want to do business with an honest establishment that will not gouge you for services you don't want or need. There are several options we'll explore.

If you don't know what your loved one desired, check the personal papers or will, as there's a possibility arrangements have already been made. If you don't have a copy of the will, contact the lawyer or the executor of the estate and ask if there were any special provisions or instructions concerning the decedent's burial.

The *average* price of a funeral and burial in the United States is between $8,000 and $10,000. The funeral for my father-in-law was just under $5,000 in 2005. That included everything. The decisions you make can vastly impact the price you pay. It's important to understand that the funeral is for the ones left behind.

The casket, grave marker, or memorial service does not impact the departed one, and there's no honor in spending more money than you can afford or going into debt for the sake of appearances, just as there is no dishonor in choosing thought-ful, affordable options. I have never heard anyone comment on how expensive the casket looked or any of the decisions that were made. Every comment I have heard has been about the service and whether or not it honored the deceased.

With that in mind, make choices you can afford. After the service, the casket, the liner, and any other thing you chose will never be seen again, so don't feel pressured to choose the most expensive or most elaborate unless you just want to and can eas-ily afford it. Many expenses came up later, and we were very thankful we didn't overspend on the burial and service.

The price ranges I will share are the result of my recent re-search in my home state of Colorado and online.

The law requires that all funeral homes and cemeteries allow you to bring in headstones, caskets, and everything needed, so if you have the energy and prefer to shop around for better prices, a reputable funeral home will not attempt to discourage that. We trusted our funeral director, and she didn't pressure us to buy anything. We purchased everything from the funeral home she represented and didn't shop around. At the time, we didn't even know shopping around was an option.

Options for Your Loved One's Remains

Burial in a Casket

Caskets range in price from a pine box costing around $300 to a very expensive casket costing $8,000 or more.

Caskets can contain embroidered fabric liners decorated with items the deceased loved or a shelf to display items or pho-tos that were important to the deceased. Caskets are made of everything from softwood to oak, pine, or even 18-20 gauge steel. There are options that include engraved or cast symbols on the inside or outside of the casket. There are even caskets made for very large people. An important side note here is that the casket will be seen for only a few hours through teary eyes, so be careful to not be talked into something you don't need or want, especially something you can't afford. There will be a large selection, so be sure the casket you choose is what you want and within your budget. In one instance, I remember hearing of a family who bought a white casket and then provided markers so friends and family of the deceased could write messages at the funeral.

> *He will swallow up death forever! The Sovereign LORD will wipe away all tears.*
> —Isa. 25:8, NLT

Grave liners range in price from $700 to $10,000.

In most areas of the United States, state or local law does not require a container—a grave liner—to surround the casket in the grave. However, many cemeteries require that you have such a container so that the grave will not give way and cause a dangerous sinkhole. A grave liner, outer burial container, or burial vault will satisfy these requirements. Made of concrete, which is the least expensive, to bronze, which is expensive, the liner can be elaborate or simple. Remember—no one sees it. It is not necessary that it be waterproof or even water resistant. If one is required, don't feel pressured into buying something fancy.

Remember: your loved one left his or her body at the moment of death. Take heart, though; Christ has overcome death for those who believe on Him.

In some cemeteries, plots are available that allow members of a family to be buried in two-tiered or three-tiered graves. In these cemetery plots, the body of the first person to die will be buried in a vault at the bottom, and the next two will be buried on top of the first. It saves ground space and cost. Be sure to ask what the cost will be for burying those who die later.

> Let not your heart be troubled;
> you believe in God, believe also in Me.
> In My Father's house are many mansions;
> if it were not so, I would have told you.
> I go to prepare a place for you.
> And if I go and prepare a place for you,
> I will come again and receive you to Myself;
> that where I am, there you may be also.
> —*John 14:1-4, NKJV*

Embalming

Embalming has a restorative effect on human remains that makes an open casket possible at the service and allows friends and family to view the body during the visitation and funeral.

Specialized college training is required for mortuary science students. Embalming a body makes it possible to delay the funeral, thus allowing time for family members living far away to be included in the service. If the body is cremated or a closed casket service is chosen, embalming is not necessary. Law does not require embalming in any state. Don't let the funeral director talk you into something you do not want or need.

In my research for this book, I asked dozens of people how they felt about the experience of viewing the body of their deceased friend or loved one. In many cases, those people said that seeing the embalmed body of the person they loved unsettled them.

One person said, "I wish I hadn't looked. I would rather remember my dad full of life instead of frozen in death."

One person said that she wanted to see him one more time

so badly that how he looked didn't matter to her. A few others said they found comfort in seeing their loved one, because seeing the body made the death seem real to them. For some, the embalmed body gave them a feeling of closure.

Since many of us live far from our families, we often receive the news of the death of a loved one by a phone call. In these cases, viewing the body might lend a sense of reality. No one—especially children—should be forced to view or touch the person or be pressured to kiss the person, as one grandmother forced a child to do at the child's mother's funeral.

Many of the folks I interviewed were eager to tell me of their awful experience seeing their deceased loved one in the casket at the funeral. It seemed that the younger the deceased person, the stronger the negative feelings toward viewing the body.

Blessed are the peacemakers, for they will be called sons of God.

—Matt. 5:9

If you decide to embalm your loved one, or if someone in the decision-making role wants to embalm the body, or your person left instructions to be embalmed, then consider placing the coffin where the attendees at the funeral can choose whether or not they wish to view the body.

Be very respectful of the wishes of other family members as you discuss these choices. Try to be a calming, understanding influence as your family makes this and other important decisions.

My middle son attended his paternal great-grandmother's funeral when he was about three years old. As we entered the church, I was carrying him. The open casket was stationed immediately inside the front door of the church, so there was no choice but to pass it as we entered the building. We were face-to-face with my grandmother's body, whether we wanted to be or not. We attended the service, shared a meal with family and friends, visited with cousins, and the kids had run around the churchyard for hours. As we got into our van for the long ride home, I had barely snapped everyone into their car seats when Matthew looked up at me with an almost angry face. His dark brown eyes seemed darker under his furrowed brow. I said, "Did you have fun with your cousins, Matthew?"

He answered, still looking at me intently, "I just have one question." He paused for a second, "Who was that lady laying in the box?"

I felt terrible. He didn't know her. He was so little, and she lived far away and had advanced Alzheimer's. At the time, we had three sons under the age of five. I had explained that we were going to a funeral for Grandpa Glen's mom. I had not, however, imagined that he would actually have to look at her body. He talked about her for several weeks. That is why I say that if you are embalming your loved one, be sure to locate the coffin in a place where visitors—especially children, at their parents' discretion—have a choice of whether or not they want to view the body.

Some folks have a viewing time, and if someone has a need to see the person one last time, he or she can come, and then the casket is closed for the funeral. That gives everyone some options. The best arrangement for a viewing that I have seen was a two- to three-hour time period the evening before the funeral. This eliminates the chance that anyone will inadvertently walk into the room and see the body of his or her loved one.

Remember: a funeral is for the ones left behind, so being respectful of everyone's needs in the grieving process is very important. I interviewed one dear person who said she just could not do the cremation thing, so she and the family felt embalming and the casket were their only options.

If you choose burial in a casket, and you don't feel the need to view your loved one's body, you can have a closed casket service with no viewing. You'll save the expense of the embalming and will not need to schedule a viewing. Again, don't let the funeral director tell you that it's required or even necessary.

With that said, I want to put in a word of defense of the funeral directors. I know five or six funeral directors personally. Each one is a compassionate, loving person who has the best interests of the families of the deceased at heart. Being a funeral director is a hard job, and most do not play on the grief of their clients. Quite the contrary, they are good listeners who work to meet the needs of the families they work with. Most times, the funeral is the beginning of the grieving process; just preparing for it has many healing qualities.

Embalming Procedure

I witnessed an embalming as part of my research. Basically, the blood of the deceased is removed from the body and replaced with formaldehyde. The technician also works to make the person look as much as possible as he or she looked in life. Many I interviewed bemoaned the fact that their dad's hair was parted on the wrong side or their mother's makeup was all wrong. These things were quite upsetting to the people I spoke with.

Typically, the family supplies a favorite outfit for the person to wear, but garments are available to purchase for that purpose. This is called "casketing." Makeup is applied, usually in accordance with the family's wishes and instructions, and the hair is styled to look as close as possible to the way it was worn in life. If the person wore glasses, it's the family's decision whether or not to put the glasses on the body. The body is put into the casket, and the cloth lining, garments, and other items are carefully arranged to look nice. The body is then ready for the viewing and funeral service. The embalmed body is kept cool.

The embalmer I watched was very respectful of the body and careful in her work.

Cremation

Cremation is the process of taking the human remains after death and turning them into ashes or "cremains" by incineration. Since a large percentage of the human body is water, cremation is simply a process of evaporation. It speeds along nature's natural process of turning a body back to dust.

The staff at the crematorium I visited was very kind and helpful. They were very respectful of the person's body and the family's wishes, and—most important to me—they were not judgmental. They view their jobs as ministry to the hurting.

I had to get special permission to watch, and I didn't know the person who had died. Had it been someone I was close to, I'm certain I would not have wanted to be there.

The furnace that does the cremation reminded me of a big kiln lined with bricks. The door opened like a big industrial oven.

Lord, Thank you that you have the wisdom we need for all the decisions we're required to make. Please lead us, and guide our choices regarding the remains of the one we loved so much.

Help us to keep our eyes on you and our hearts at peace.

In Jesus' name we pray. Amen.

Very few bodies are cremated in an actual casket. There's no need to purchase a coffin for someone who is being cremated. If there will be an open casket at the funeral service and your

If any of you lacks wisdom, he should ask God, who gives generously to all without finding fault, and it will be given to him.

—James 1:5

loved one is being cremated, rental caskets are available to use for the service.

Jewelry, glasses, or other personal articles will be removed and returned to the family. If the family doesn't want these items, they'll be left with the body. Almost anything can be cremated with the loved one. Some families find comfort in adding their pet's cremains or a favorite item the person loved. For instance, a favorite fishing pole, photographs, a note from the loved ones—simply writing a letter to be placed with the body can sometimes be good therapy. Others include the deceased's favorite Bible or other book. It's a matter of the family members deciding what will best bring them closure. Laying to rest someone who meant a lot to us is very important in our healing from the loss. The funeral and activities surrounding the death serve as the starting point for the healing process.

The last item to be put into the crematorium is a small metal tag to identify the cremains later. This is how a person can be reasonably certain that the cremains of his or her loved one are the cremains received in the urn or container.

After I watched a cremation, some of my friends shared with me that they thought it would be a gruesome experience. I, however, took great comfort in seeing it, because now I'm certain that once a person dies, he or she is no longer in that earthly shell. The body we inhabit while we live here is exchanged for a new one with no illnesses or pain. A wonderful affirmation for the believer is found in Rev. 21:4: "He will wipe every tear from their eyes. There will be no more death or mourning or crying or pain, for the old order of things has passed away."

Options for Disposition of the Body

Headstone ($400 to several thousand dollars)

Headstones mark the grave of the departed, regardless of whether you choose to bury your loved one's cremains or bury the body in a casket.

Headstones range in price from $400 to $500 for a plain horizontal marker that lies flush with the ground, up to several thousand dollars for other styles. The cost depends on how elaborate the marker is. Many options are available, such as ceramic portraits or photos, and large, standing, marble markers with engraving on the plate. Cast images or a vase for flowers can be added for a price.

Markers are sometimes vandalized. The metal used for the vases on headstones is so valuable that thousands have been stolen recently. Ask the funeral director if the cemetery carries insurance for such things.

Burial in a Mausoleum ($6,400 to $157,500)

Also referred to as a tomb, crypt, or burial chamber, a mausoleum is a building for entombment above ground. Some parts of North America are at sea level or below, making it problematic to bury below ground. Mausoleums can be used for either cremains or the body. It can be a single structure for one person or a larger structure for the whole family.

Burial in a Crypt Designed for the Remains of Many ($250 to $1,500)

Some memorial parks offer crypts for the remains of more than one body, and some do not. Especially for cremains, it's a cost-effective option if one doesn't want to keep the cremains or bury them with a marker. Usually a marker plaque can be placed on the niche within the crypt that contains the remains of the loved one.

Church Burial of Cremains

Some churches maintain a memorial garden in which a member's cremains can be placed. There may be a nominal charge, but some churches don't charge. If you don't know whether or not the church your loved one belongs to offers this service, ask.

Cremation ($800 to $5,500)

The cremation can be done in a wooden cremation casket suitable for a service prior to the cremation ($300-$400) or a cardboard container ($100-$200). The total fee for a direct, or immediate, cremation in an alternative container is around $1,500.

Funeral Depot at <www.funeraldepot.com> has the least expensive container I found online.

Cremains Buried

Many choose to bury their loved one's cremains with a grave marker. When my father-in-law died, we purchased a half lot in the cemetery, and my mother-in-law's cremains will be buried with his in that half lot. Take into account the feelings of other family members as to whether or not you wish to purchase a grave marker or headstone.

Donation of the Body to Science

Donation of the body to science can be prearranged through medical schools or done after the death. A fee may apply for transporting the remains to the school from the place of death or the mortuary. Some universities have strict requirements that must be met that necessitate some prearrangement. There may also be rules about how soon after death the body may be delivered to the school, and also qualifications concerning the condition of the body, such as previous surgeries and the nature of the surgeries. My mother-in-law has chosen to donate her body to science then cremated and buried with Mel's cremains.

Embalmed Body for Service with a Closed Casket

No law in the United States makes embalming mandatory, so don't allow your family to be pressured into embalming by the funeral home if a viewing is not desired. If the body is going to be shipped a long distance, however, embalming requirements could apply even if a viewing will not take place.

Embalming the Body for a Service Followed by Cremation

If you plan a viewing, embalming is a requirement even if cremation follows. Your funeral director will give you the details, the pricing, and any other pertinent information. Be sure to ask questions if you don't understand everything.

Embalming for Viewing ($400 to $1,000)

This involves embalming and preparing the body for viewing, such as dressing the body, doing the hair and makeup, and other procedures. If the embalmer provides the burial garments, if restoration or reconstruction work on the body is required, or if the body has been autopsied, the cost increases.

Organ and Tissue Donation

Each person who chooses to become an organ and tissue donor may save the lives of as many as eight people and enhance the lives of as many as 50 others. By joining the registry while you're alive, you help your family by having made that decision, thereby relieving them of having to make it upon your death.

Being on the donor registry does not affect one's quality of health care; the recovery team is completely separate from the medical team treating the individual. The organ recovery team isn't called in until the medical team has done everything possible to save the patient.

If you have questions regarding organ and tissue donation for yourself or for a loved one, visit <www.donor-awareness.org>, or call the Donor Awareness Council at 303-388-8605 or 1-888-388-8605.

Spreading Your Loved One's Cremains in a Place He or She Loved

There's no charge for spreading your loved one's cremains, but there are precautions to be considered.

Many people ask that their cremains be spread over a place they loved—a lake, the ocean, a mountain vista, or a garden. If you choose this option, be very careful. Cremains are not ashes, as they seem, but they are calcified bone fragments and are quite dense. There have been cases reported of folks going up in an airplane to spread the cremains, and when they threw the ashes out the open hatch of the airplane, the ashes blew back into their faces. If the cremains are inhaled, the results can be fatal, and if they blow into the engine of a small plane, it may stall.

So be careful about your plans to spread the cremains. Also, be sure to check before you scatter. In some places it's illegal to scatter cremains without getting prior permission.

Keeping Cremains in an Urn or Container

Keepsake urns are available from reasonably priced to quite expensive. The cremains can even be put into several separate containers so that the ashes are divided among the family. No regulations apply as to what sort of container ashes must be kept in, so you can keep them in anything you choose. The memorial park I visited said they provide a black plastic container at a very low price, and they also have more expensive containers available at varying prices.

Remember . . .

There are many decisions to make in a short amount of time when a loved one passes away, and grieving survivors may feel ill-equipped to deal with so much. Remember: the person who has died no longer cares what happens to his or her "old house." Do what brings you and other family members the most comfort. If your loved one left instructions of what he or she prefers, it would be respectful to follow those instructions as closely as possible.

When my father-in-law passed away, he had not said a word to anyone about what he preferred. Even when he suffered from recurrent cancer, he would not discuss it. In fact, we often speculate that he had decided he would never die. The trouble with that thinking is that it leaves the survivors with a lot of important decisions to make at a time when they're least able to handle the stress.

Just before I went to make his arrangements, his wife of more than 57 years said she would like for him to be cremated. I was not legally his next of kin, so I was extremely careful to do what she wanted. If you're helping plan a service and are not next of kin, you must be careful to not overstep your boundaries as well. A form is available for a person to complete to designate someone other than the next of kin to be responsible for the arrangements.

When my friend Dana's mother passed away, all four of her daughters were surprised to learn that their mother had selected and paid for the flowers, the casket, and prepaid to have it shipped to their hometown. After the funeral service, the entire family and extended family were invited to a restaurant they all loved to have a meal together. The tab had been prepaid by their mother. What an amazing parting gift she gave her family. I hope I'm as good to my family.

For what it's worth, this is what we did when my father-in-law passed away. Papa was cremated, and we had a headstone placed over the gravesite that had a vase on it to hold flowers. When the cemetery was vandalized, the vase on his headstone was stolen, and that was very upsetting to my mother-in-law. If I had it to do over again, and it was just me deciding, I would have brought his cremains home and spread them in the garden, in our yard, or on Mt. Evans. He loved gardens, and the cost of the grave seems like a lot of money to spend, especially since he's not even there. I want to emphasize, though, that if someone close to your loved one wants to embalm and bury the body in a casket or make other arrangements for the cremains, be sensitive to their needs and careful about who you hire to handle the service.

The following is a list of costs as they were in May 2005 in the area where we live.

Direct Cremation with Memorial Service ($1,648)

Direct cremation without any attendant rites or ceremonies

includes transfer of the remains from the place of death and shelter of the remains; consultation with the family; preparation and filing of necessary authorization and permits; recording of vital statistics; local telephone service; and basic services and overhead. It did not include a visitation.

Service Preparations (Approximately $150)

In addition to the $150 for the service preparations, I spent another $150 making the slide show and poster board for Mel's service. The funeral home didn't supply any of this. We also copied a poem written by Aunt Joy onto decorative paper to put in the order of service.

One-Half Plot to Bury Cremains ($750)

A fee of $750 included the one-half plot to have Mel's cremains buried in and later those of his wife.

Marker ($1,786)

A small bronze marker with names and dates cost $1,786. It is flush with the ground and has a picture of trees and mountains cast into it.

Opening and Closing of Ground ($325)

A fee of $325 was charged for burying the cremains and placing the headstone in the ground.

Use of Two Industrial Coffee Pots for the Service ($20)

We used these to serve those who attended the service.

10 Death Certificates ($69)

I suggest you get 25 death certificates. Many of the places

that request them will accept only originals, and it's less expensive to order them all at one time.

Register Book ($42)

You can buy your own guest register book, but the one the funeral home offered matched the programs, and it was one less thing for us to think about. I've seen lovely books used for guests to sign that weren't designed specifically for that purpose. It's also nice to have a basket of some type near the register book for condolence cards that attendees may bring.

Order of Service Folders ($57 for 100)

In my research I've seen some beautiful programs that cost a little more that were very honoring to the memory of the deceased person.

Total: $4,847

Other costs not included in the total were for paper products, cookies, and drinks we bought for the service. As it turned out, many of the attendees brought cookies or other finger foods. We didn't know what to expect, so we purchased some ourselves.

I asked Cindy at Evergreen Memorial Park what other expenses we might expect. She said it's customary to offer an honorarium to everyone who participates in or officiates at the service.

The Church (Most churches have a set fee for using the facility)
Pastor ($90 to $250)
Organist, Pianist, Soloist ($100 each)
Sound Technician ($75 to $100)
Nursery Workers (Hourly according to number of children)

Janitorial Staff (Might be included in church fee)
Bagpiper or Harpist ($100, or may have set fee)

3 ～ THE OBITUARY AND NOTIFICATION OF THE DEATH

Let us therefore come boldly to the throne of grace,
that we may obtain mercy and find grace to help in time of need.
—Heb. 4:16, NKJV

Writing an obituary is much like the job a reporter does. It is a means of conveying important information about the deceased. You might have to go on a fact-finding mission before starting to write the obituary. I'm not sure I could even write my own without looking at my résumé. Many funeral homes will take care of writing and placing the obituary in the newspaper and will have a list of questions they'll ask you before writing it.

The cost of placing the obituary in a newspaper varies greatly. A friend shared with me that to have her mother's placed in a New York newspaper was $400, while a much lengthier obituary with a photo was only $30 to place in the newspaper of the town where she grew up. Many papers charge by the word or line, so if money is an issue, be brief. You can post an online obituary to share with friends and family later.

My friend Sue put her mother's high school photograph in the hometown paper, and many of her mother's high school classmates contacted Sue. They expressed how great it was to see that photo in the paper, because they recognized her right away. Consider placing the obituary in newspapers serving areas where the person formerly lived. Be sure to clip a copy when it's published so you can send it to friends and relatives. My aunt copied the obituary onto pretty paper and handed it out with the program at my cousin Rick's service.

Be sure to check with the newspaper for length restrictions. The best time to place the obituary is a few days before the funeral is to be held. Sunday is an especially good day to post an obituary.

In the first paragraph include the following:

Name

Age

Address

Date of death

Place of death

Cause or suspected cause of death

In the second paragraph include the following:

Date of birth

Birthplace

Parents' names

Educational accomplishments

Military service if applicable

Which war or conflict he or she served in

Where he or she was stationed if overseas

Marriages

History of where he or she lived

In the third paragraph include the following:

Elementary and high school attended

Post-high school education

Degrees earned

Licenses held

In the fourth paragraph include the following:

Career history

In the fifth paragraph include the following:

Church affiliation and service to the church

Civic memberships (community, government, or town)

Fraternal or club memberships

With all the above include positions, special projects done, and offices held.

Hobbies (Was he a fisherman? Was she a quilter?)

Other interests

In the sixth paragraph include the names of the following:

Parents, if living

Spouse

Children and their spouses and city and state of residence

Grandchildren

Great-grandchildren

Great-great-grandchildren

Grandparents

Brothers

Sisters

Nephews

Nieces

Cousins

Close friends

List family that preceded him or her in death, such as spouse, parents, children, grandchildren, great-grandchildren, brothers, and sisters.

In the seventh paragraph include the following:

> List of memorial funds that have been established. Tell where memorial contributions may be sent, but do not say "In lieu of flowers." Someone may really want to send flowers, and an arrangement or two at the service is nice. Many folks send baskets of flowering plants that may be given to special friends or family after the service. If someone lives far away and cannot attend, he or she may find great comfort in sending something for the service. Mel's sister Joy and brother Wayne could not attend his funeral, so they sent a beautiful bird bath to put in the garden right outside the office window that my mother-in-law uses every day. It was a lovely gift to her. Torrey, a friend, sent a colossal geranium. We had it for the whole summer and into the fall.

In the last paragraph include the names of people or organizations you wish to thank for care given to the deceased.

If the deceased is a child or young person, most of this would not apply. You could also include attributes that person possessed, things he or she loved. For sample obituaries, you could go to the local newspaper or the *New York Times* online site as the obituaries in that paper are usually very well written.

Many people read the obituaries every day, even if they haven't lost someone. The above is just an outline. Be sure to omit or include whatever best fits your loved one's life. The order of the middle paragraphs does not matter, but the first and seventh are usually easier to read if they're in chronological order. Check <www.legacy.com>, a Web site connected with many newspapers that allows people to send notes of condolences or encouragements via the Internet. For security purposes, do not post your street address. It's best to include only city and state.

Be sure to e-mail people in your loved one's address book online. We made many of the people who were close to Mel aware of his death by sending an e-mail to those in his online address book. Most of his extended family and many of his friends live far away, so we did not expect them to come to his service. But by notifying them right away, many of them were able to contact his wife and give her comfort in her time of extreme loss. It's a cost- and time-effective means of letting folks know. Be sure to announce the death in your loved one's church bulletin also. He or she may have had a profound impact on someone whom neither your loved one nor you are aware of.

4 ∿ THE EULOGY— A TRIBUTE

Hear my prayer, O LORD, And let my cry come to You.
Do not hide Your face from me in the day of my trouble;
Incline Your ear to me; In the day that I call, answer me speedily.
—Ps. 102:1-2, NKJV

Being asked to present a tribute to the deceased is an honor re-served for closest friends or family members. A eulogy is a spo-ken expression to celebrate the life of the one who has died. If you are asked to deliver a eulogy, you may discover that you find healing in the process of writing and rehearsing it. My oldest son, now 17, was very upset that he didn't get to say good-bye to his grandfather when he passed away. He found that writing and delivering the eulogy gave him his chance to say good-bye and begin the healing process. As you compile thoughts about your loved one, here are some questions that might help you get started:

- How did you meet him or her? How long ago?
- When did you become close?
- What are some lessons you learned from him or her?
- If you were asked to describe the person in one sentence or one word, what would it be? Was he or she passionate or energy in motion? Compassionate? What best describes your person?
- Was there something that struck you about him or her?
- What will you miss about this person?

- What is something you appreciate or admire?
- Can you remember some funny thing that happened?
- Was there a time when he or she made you feel really good about yourself?
- What was one of the happiest times you shared with the person?
- What did he or she do that made you laugh?

As you organize your thoughts, remember that the goal is to bring your person's good characteristics to the front of everyone's mind and give them something to walk away with. If you can, bring up little nuances, funny thoughts, favorite sayings. For example, Papa always said, "If a job is worth doing, it's worth doing right" and "The generation that comes after me should be better."

Remember funny little things the person used to say. When asked where he got something or where he was going shopping, my father-in-law would reply simply, "Here and there." When we asked what the plan was for a particular day, he usually replied "This and that." Every person who knew him would smile at that memory. Those were his signature lines.

Talk about what legacy your loved one leaves for the next generation. For example, Ron Lint paraphrased Prov. 31, giving examples of how Linda modeled that passage to everyone who interfaced with her. Just reading it made me aspire to be a better wife and mother—a better everything.

Suggested Details for the Eulogy

- Place and date of birth
- Places lived and schools attended
- Education and diplomas or degrees received
- Places he or she traveled

- Marriage and family
- Illness/accidents/personal struggles. Give examples of how he or she overcame trials.
- Place and reason for death
- Special hobbies and volunteer positions during different periods in his or her life, such as Cub Scout leader, Sunday School teacher, Little League coach
- Traditions he or she established or followed
- What was he or she passionate about? His family was his life, or she was a visionary who could see the big picture with incredible accuracy.
- What causes did he or she rally to support? Did he or she volunteer for civic causes or charities?

If the person you are eulogizing had a hard life and suffered considerably, writing the eulogy might be more difficult. When my cousin Rick died of Huntington's disease last fall, it was after years of trial and tribulation that were difficult for him and painful to watch for those who loved him. When I was helping with his funeral, I took a scripture and compared it to him. Searching for the right scripture and pondering how he lived it out was therapy for me. I knew I couldn't stand up there and say it, so I opted to print it and mount it on an autumn-colored paper. On one side was the scripture, and the other side told of the ways he modeled the scripture. I added pressed fall leaves and laminated them for a keepsake for those who attended. My Aunt Phoebe sent them out in the thank-you cards to folks who couldn't attend the service. I will miss him. Here is my tribute to my cousin Rick:

On the front
Let us run

with endurance
the race that is
set before us,
looking unto Jesus,
the author and
finisher of our faith.
—Heb. 12:1-2, NKJV

On the back
Richard Westerman
(Rick)
2007
He endured much and
with hardly a complaint
ran the race to the end,
a race set before him that was
not of his choosing.
He believed Christ to be
the author of his faith.
It is finished.
He now resides in Glory
with the Father and Son.
For those who believe
it's not
"Good-bye"
but
"See 'ya later!"
Amen!

At my father-in-law's funeral we gave everyone the opportunity to write a short eulogy to be read by the pastor. Mel's children, his wife, and one grandson each wrote one. When the pastor read the eulogies, it was amazing to me how different Mel's impact was on each of his loved ones.

When I asked my friends to e-mail me ideas of things that had helped them during their times of loss, several of them noted that in the days before the funeral their pastor met with close friends and relatives and they sat for a time talking about the deceased. Every person who had that experience commented on how much it helped. Talking about all the wonderful times and remembering all the funny stories were healing experiences. It was a reminder that our loved one will live on in our hearts and minds as long as we can remember the things that made us love him or her. Gone from us for now, but certainly not forgotten!

In Doug Manning's book *Comforting Those Who Grieve*, he includes a chapter titled "Private Times with the Family." In that chapter he talks about the healing properties of this very practice. He writes,

These sessions will vary with each family. There is no way to predict how they will go or which direction they will take. I have sat with families who had a great deal of bitterness within the group. These are the hard ones, but these are also the ones who need these sessions the most. They need to begin the process of facing their anger, and they need to find out they are not the only ones present with negative feelings. They rarely show much anger during the session, but they do not need to do so. If they can just say they have had problems with this person, they have taken a giant step. It is now in the open. They do not need to fake their way through the funeral or the living after the funeral. The most effective private funerals I have held have been these difficult ones. I leave feeling that some have been set free. (pp 43-44)

He went on to say that if there is no hostility, these sessions are the most wonderful times of the family drawing closer together. It's then that they begin to share each other's grief.

When Papa died, our pastor came and sat with us the day before the funeral. My father-in-law was a character, to be sure, so we had a grand time telling the pastor how wonderful he made Christmas, how bossy he was, how much fun he was to hang out with, what a wonderful bridge partner he was, how he left little unexpected gifts of fresh food on the counter all the time, such as a flat of strawberries on Christmas Eve. My kids really enjoyed this time. We laughed and cried, and in the end we all slept better that night. I would highly recommend that you hold a session like this yourself if your pastor doesn't do it. It was like the Balm of Gilead for us. If you're writing a eulogy, being present for this session would be very helpful. It's especially important if you're the only one writing it for the group.

Lord, laying a loved one to rest is such a hard thing. Please give us your courage for the task ahead, and help us rest in you. In Jesus name I pray. Amen.

5 ～ THE BURIAL SERVICE

I am convinced that neither death nor life, neither angels nor demons,
neither the present nor the future, nor any powers, neither height nor
depth, nor anything else in all creation, will be able to separate us from
the love of God that is in Christ Jesus our Lord.
—Rom. 8:38-39

The burial, or internment, is often the hardest service for many. I heard of a family who did the internment in the morning, with only family present, then held the memorial service in the late afternoon. They stood around the grave and shared stories of their loved one. It was very therapeutic for them, and after the memorial service there was no rush to move to the gravesite.

At Linda's internment several men approached the grave carrying huge bouquets of colorful, helium-filled balloons, and several of the grandchildren handed out pens and little pieces of paper with a hole punched in the corner of each one. Everyone was encouraged to write a sentiment, a message, or a last farewell to Linda and attach it to a balloon. After the short ceremony committing her body to the Lord, her husband, Ron, shouted, "To my girlfriend, Linda!" and we let go of our balloons. It was a very moving, powerful moment. As we stood there watching the balloons fly away, it seemed very symbolic of releasing Linda to the Lord. I have since heard it suggested that the spouse release the only white balloon.

At the funeral of my friend Dana's mother, the younger children who didn't participate in the service wrote messages on balloons during the service, and at the gravesite they let them go. The older children wrote their messages on the way to the cemetery. She said it was terrific for the children.

My friend Sandy's family did this for their grandmother. Most of the children were small at the time, and now every time her youngest child has a helium balloon, she wants to send it to her grandma.

Some have issues releasing balloons because of environmental concerns. One family released butterflies, another ladybugs. Tailor it to your family, but there's symbolism in releasing something—letting it go. Here are some web sites with information regarding this:

<www.abutterflyrelease.com>

<www.butterflyreleasecompany.com>

<www.naturescontrol.com/ladybugs.html>

I've also heard of releasing homing pigeons at the end of the graveside service. Some families have a 21-gun salute, and a few have had a fly-by from the military.

At my cousin Rick's funeral, the pallbearers removed their boutonnieres and laid them on the coffin before we left. Again, it's all about closure.

If your family has chosen, as mine did, not to have a graveside service but you feel there's some value in the kinds of things folks do there, then after the memorial service invite the attendees to come outside and do something to commemorate the release of your loved one. You could have the whole service outside. One family had the service at their loved one's favorite picnic spot in the mountains followed by a potluck dinner. For them it was perfect. If there are cremains, they could be spread there too.

My friend Beth's father-in-law moved to Colorado to live with them. Beth and her husband were the only ones who knew him here. When he was dying at Christmastime, the family members who were in town gathered around his bed and sang Christmas songs. When he passed away the next morning, they held the service right then and there. They shared memories and told stories, even played music. She said it was very old-world and intimate. They all got to have that meaningful last look.

6 ~ A WORD TO THE BEREAVED

Be still, and know that I am God.
—Ps. 46:10

Some things this side of heaven just don't make sense to us. No platitudes or contrite sayings penetrate the pain. Sometimes rotten things happen to great people. We can't understand why they happen, we can't find rhyme or reason for them, and we certainly can't explain them. So how, then, do we proceed? How do we keep going?

We cling to our Savior and let the storm rage around us. Times like these are when the rubber of our faith meets the road. We either look to the Father to see us through, or we shake our fist at Him and curse. Some decide He must not really be up there or down here with us, or He must not really care even if He is present. Sometimes we have all these feelings on the same day. Our faith is, after all, a journey—a process. We're all works in progress. Thankfully, the Lord knows right where we are, and our anger is neither a surprise nor an affront to Him. He doesn't listen to me raging in my pain and say, "What am I going to do with that Liz Cowen Furman?" He's patient and waits for me to turn back to Him.

If you're going through that valley of the shadow of death and can't see the way to navigate, then I encourage you to pour the contents of your heart out at the foot of the Cross. Bring it all—the hurt, the anger, the guilt, the sorrow, the fear of the future, the regrets, the loneliness, the terror of the reality of what happened, your new doubt that God exists at all, the emptiness within, even the inability to care or cry anymore. Whatever you're feeling, He wants to hear it.

At my most desperate time, when I had nothing left, the tears had all been cried, the doubts had overwhelmed me, and I had pounded my pillow to oblivion, I cried out to the Lord of Lords. I curled up into a ball on my bed and said, *You can have it all.* I was overwhelmed by my loss of hope. In that moment, it was as if God himself reached out to me and lifted me into His lap. The verse "As I was with Moses, so I will be with you; I will never leave you nor forsake you" (Josh. 1:5) came to mind. After a few hours, a glimmer of hope began to return.

This coming to the end of myself was not caused by the death of someone I loved but rather the result of my own bad choices, the death of a dream. Whatever leads us to the end of our rope, God is there to rescue us from falling off the end into the abyss. His promises to be with us always, even unto the end of the age, are found throughout Scripture. "I am with you always, to the very end of the age" (Matt. 28:20).

The stories of God's faithfulness, miracles, and amazing grace that come out of tragic events we're forced to face show that God can and does take rotten things and bring good out of the ashes. In our pain, we often don't want good out of the ashes—we want our loved one back. He is still God.

Knowing that God has everything under control—even if I can't see it—has become the rock on which I stand. That doesn't mean I don't cry my eyes out at the loss of someone precious to me. It simply means that I trust Him to see me through. I know that God's desire is to show mercy and kindness to all who trust

Him. I'm comforted by this verse: "The LORD is close to the brokenhearted and saves those who are crushed in spirit" (Ps. 34:18).

Granted, what's best for us and what we desire are sometimes at odds. So in times of loss and grieving, though we see through a glass darkly, we trust His heart. In that great song by Wayne Watson, "Trust His Heart," we're reminded that His character is unchanging and that evil is not caused by Him, though He permits it.

I recently heard Joni Eareckson Tada on the radio say, "God permits what he hates—to accomplish what He loves." What He loves is being in relationship with us, and He has promised to see us through the tough times.

In his book *Comforting Those Who Grieve*, Doug Manning writes:

> Somehow I overlooked the natural process of the grief experience. Grief lasts much longer than most people expect.
>
> [During this] period, there are peaks and valleys. There will be an intense peak at an anniversary, birthday, holiday, and most Sundays. For some reason, there will usually be a peak just before the two-year mark. (p. 13)

My occupational therapist said to me after a closed-head injury resulting from a car accident, "If you broke your arm and it was in a cast, no one would ask you to row a boat or lift a bale of hay until the injury had healed." But with head injuries—and broken hearts, I've discovered—some people expect us to bounce right back and get on with life. Since there's nothing visible to mark the injury, it's easy to forget that the injury is still there, still healing. Mr. Manning suggests that if we don't allow ourselves to grieve and we act better before we really are, we'll carry around unresolved grief that can be deadly.

I read many books about the stages of grief as I researched

this book. Some say there are four, some say ten, and any number between, but suffice it to say there are definitely things we must process before we heal. I'll quickly outline the major issues I found in these books and my own experiences with the grieving process so you can at least know what to expect. At the end of this book I've listed some great reading suggestions. I encourage you to go there and read as many as possible.

Stages of Grief

Denial or shock. However you label it, a period comes following a loss in which we operate in survival mode. Some describe not even remembering the first months or even a year after a huge loss. My mother-in-law said that the second Christmas without her husband of nearly 60 years was much worse than the first. The first one went by without her, but by the time the second Christmas came, she was aware, and it hit hard. Her Father Christmas had gone home for good.

Sorrow and sadness. Reality. Finality. This is the most difficult time. The realization that you will never see the person again this side of heaven has hit. The finality of death often comes as a surprise. You begin to stop expecting your loved one to return from a trip or to walk in the door. This is the stage that most often hurts physically. The chest tightens, we feel weak, sometimes it feels hard to breathe, and we fear we can't go forward. A permanent lump is in our throat, and we cry at the drop of a hat. Some want to sleep, because fatigue is palpable, while others stay as busy as possible to avoid thinking about the loss. This is the time that's the most difficult for those who love us. They want to take our pain away, but there is no way anyone can. In fact, it's part of the healing process. We must walk through it.

Anger. This one is scary to many of us as well as to those who love us. When we get to the bottom of our pain, we get mad. Maybe it's that old fight-or-flight reaction. We can't believe this could happen—that a loving God would allow us to hurt so fiercely—and we become fierce. Some get mad at God, some get mad at the doctor, some get mad at themselves. Others focus their anger on the pastor or well-meaning friends who really don't understand. Some even get mad at the funeral director. This anger is natural, and it's another part of the process. There really isn't anything to say that will help. Just listening is the best thing. If you're in this stage, you might find yourself needing to talk. You may surprise yourself by telling a complete stranger the whole story.

Healing, resolution, recovery. This is the last stage in the process, when the person decides to get better, finding that he or she is able to handle that which was terrifying before: cleaning out the loved one's closet, going out alone. The pain eases a bit, and the memories that caused severe pain a few months ago begin to be treasured remembrances of someone well-loved. It will never be the same without the loved one, but the grieving person begins to believe that he or she will be able to go on.

A very important side note here is that these are not necessarily experienced in order or even one at a time. A grieving person may experience several stages of grief on the same day, maybe even a couple at the same time. The most important thing to remember is that grieving is hard work, and it takes time. I would recommend that everyone who has experienced a significant loss get into a grief recovery group. One of the most important things that helps in the recovery is having someone to talk to, someone to hear your story. A well-run recovery group can meet those needs to tell your story and have someone really listen. Sometimes talking is the best therapy. I also want to mention that journaling has been one of the best tools I've used in the process. The result also gave me a chronicle of what I went through and how it felt.

When Curtis Graves's family was killed in an accident, Curtis stood at the funeral and said, "The reason I'm able to stand before you today and have any hope of going on is my relationship with Jesus and the prayers of the faithful; you know that I am nothing without my family." Most of us could not breathe at that point and couldn't stop our tears. He encouraged us to love our families well and to not sweat the small stuff that he said he had been sweating just days before. He said, "This is something I can't macho my way through." It felt as if our legs had been swept out from under us. Words can't express it.

Wake-up call? Yes! We can surely learn from Curtis's words of encouragement and his reliance on the only one who can heal broken hearts.

Until you're able to reach out to Him to help you, just rest in the truth that He's there. In dark, scary times it may seem nearly impossible to know for sure that the God of the universe cares about His children. Until the tears are cried out and you've reached the end of your own strength, know that He's waiting for you.

In an e-mail from my friend who lost his dear wife, he wrote,

You asked me how I am doing. Liz, I am profoundly, palpably, and miserably sad. I am so lonely. I don't even remember not being married. I miss her so much. I am on the verge of tears most of every day, but I realized I had two major choices to make: (1) I could wither, be permanently depressed and depressing to all with whom I come in contact, be profoundly bitter, blame God, and generally be no good to anyone. (2) I can hold on to Jesus, look to the future, serve Him, not let the unanswered questions of life overshadow that which I know—that Jesus is Lord—and I can go forward. Liz, I choose the latter.

There will probably still be days when he chooses option one, but holding onto Jesus is always a good choice. Grieving takes time, and giving yourself the time you need to heal from a broken heart is the best thing you can do for yourself and all who love you. Remember—it takes every person a different amount of time to heal. Give your heart the time it needs, and cling to the one who has the power to heal your broken heart.

One last thing—during these dark times I encourage you to journal your feelings, because when you've healed, you won't remember all you felt. Journaling has incredible healing powers to those who hurt.

Driving down the road shortly after Mel's passing, I wondered how long it would take before all the memories of the fun times with him would stop causing me pain and become happy memories of someone I loved. Who has died, how long you were together, how deeply you loved him or her—all factor in to how long it will take for the pain to subside. For me it was several months, but once in a while, nearly three years later, I'm still caught off-guard when I cry at the memory of something I miss about him. He was my bridge partner. He and I and my mother-in-law and my husband solved the world's problems during those bridge sessions. Sometimes the kids even joined us for a game of bridge. I so miss that.

Lord, please come and show us the way. The pain from this loss is palpable. Help us rest in you. Give us your perspective, and show us how to proceed. In Jesus name we pray. Amen.

7 ⌒ HOW YOU CAN HELP SOMEONE WHO IS GRIEVING

*Dear children, let us not love with words or tongue
but with actions and in truth.*
—1 John 3:18

If you know someone who's going through the loss of a loved one, here are a few practical ideas to help.

The second most important thing you can do for someone who's grieving is to be a willing listener. Show up, even if you don't know what to say. A big part of the healing process of grieving a loss is talking it through. You really don't have to say much—"I'm so sorry." Then let him or her take it from there.

The *most* important thing you can do to help someone in pain is to pray for him or her. Pray that God will give the bereaved comfort, listen, and be with him or her during this hard time. And don't stop praying for a long time to come. Pray often, not just the "Have a good day" prayer, but go deeper. Ask the Holy Spirit to show you how to pray specifically for the person and then do it regularly.

Send a card. The cards streaming into our house after Mel's passing were a great encouragement to all of us, but I think they were especially meaningful for Muff, his wife. She read them all as they arrived, but it wasn't until a year or two later that she read them again, and they were even more powerful.

If a child in the family has experienced a loss, send a card just to the child. Children are often forgotten grievers when a family is going through the crisis of losing someone.

Try to send a card each week for a year. Long after the attention is gone and everyone seems to have forgotten the loss, it's nice to know someone recognizes that life is not going along as usual. I've sent postcards while traveling to make sure the person got the weekly card.

Be sure to acknowledge the birthday of the lost loved one.

Call, visit, or send a card on the first anniversary of his or her passing. We all took Muff out to dinner at Mel's favorite restaurant on that day.

Go to one of those places where meals can be made ahead and frozen, and stock the freezer. It will be welcome later when all the church ladies discontinue the wonderful meals they often bring in after a death.

Weeks after the death, bring a meal over.

Call often to offer your ear. Don't give advice unless you're asked. Depending on how close to the person you are, take him or her out to lunch, or bring it in occasionally.

Plant flowers that may have come for the services, or bring some in to a spot that will bring joy.

Do something in the fallen loved one's honor. The middle school boys' basketball team arranged to fix up the outside basketball court in honor of Cameron, a teammate who had lived, eaten, and slept basketball before his death.

If it's allowed, plant something or put a bench near the gravesite.

Comfort food is always appreciated. Be sure to send fresh fruit, as it's so good for us. Also, be sure to ask about allergies, diet restrictions, and likes and dislikes.

Go with your friend—or offer to drive—to order copies of the death certificate. We needed 20 original copies but ordered only 10 to begin with, because we didn't know. Sometimes the funeral home will order them for you initially, so be sure to get plenty. It's cheaper in the long run to order all you'll need.

Commission a portrait of the lost loved one, and give it to the ones left behind. Careful with the timing of this one—it might need to come later.

Offer to help with the endless paperwork and notifications needed in the weeks and months after the funeral. Here are some examples of what might be needed:

- Cancel magazine subscriptions, especially if no one in the home is interested in the subject matter. Also cancel alumni notifications and newsletters.
- To remove the name of the deceased from marketing lists, go to <https://www.ims-dm.com/cgi/ddnc.php>.
- Notify folks who send mail to him or her, such as libraries or fundraisers or newsletters.
- Offer to help organize bills and go through files to find an account for all stocks, bonds, bills, and insurance policies. Be sure your help is wanted—don't push. It would be especially important if the person left was not the one who handled the family finances.

Come over and clean the house and water the plants.

Weed the garden if necessary.

Offer to pick up something—milk or bendy straws for an injured person who can't sit up to drink, or whatever he or she needs from the store when you're going.

Stop by to give a hug and an offer for anything. No need to stay long, just to give reassurance that you're there. When our friends the Blongs were in a car wreck, the youngest of their four sons was killed, and all the others were injured. I popped in several times as I passed by on my way home. Cindy, the mom, later said, "No one else came. It was as if we had the plague." Even if you don't know what to say, just go. I was shaking in fear the first time I walked up to the door, but I had to go!

Arrange for a massage therapist to come to their house a few times. All that stress, pain, and anxiety needs to be worked out of those head, neck, and back muscles. A friend said this was very helpful.

Give the person a copy of *Devotions for the Brokenhearted,* by Robin Prince Monroe. Give *Jonathan, You Left Too Soon,* by David Biebel, if he or she lost a child.

Send little gifts of encouragement. The postal service has delivered many a package of encouragement. Little things, not expensive things, or handmade things that make the person smile are very appreciated. Seasonal items such as a pressed autumn leaf or a twig of bittersweet are good. It's great to receive anything in the mail that isn't a bill, an ad, or bad news.

Give a blank, lined journal to a griever so he or she can pour thoughts and feelings onto the pages.

Write or print a favorite verse on pretty paper, add a pressed flower or fall leaf, laminate it, and send it as a day-brightener. Good choices would be Ps. 91; Phil. 4:13; 2 Cor. 4:8-9. Add a magnet on the back to attach it to a locker or refrigerator.

If the person is elderly or lives alone, arrange for delivery by Meals on Wheels, or organize a group from church or work to bring meals a couple times a week for a few months.

Send flowers or a plant. I send plants instead of flowers six months after the funeral or on the anniversary of the loved one's passing.

Do "100 days of prayer" for the person left behind. Keep a journal of your prayers, and give it to the person at a later time. Be sure to date each entry so he or she can look back to see how your prayers made a difference. It's nice to know that someone is praying for us.

If the person has children and a birthday comes up, offer to have the party at your house and plan it. It's really difficult to plan a party when all you want to do is cry.

Whatever your role in the life of the grieving, there are things you can do to encourage and lift up that person or persons. Be assured no act of kindness will be wasted. Even if you never hear how it impacted them, keep up the good work.

What Not to Say or Do

A little side note here of some things *not* to say. The folks I interviewed while writing this book said there were things said to them that were offensive. When we had our miscarriage, when Papa died, and when Rick died, several folks said some goofy things to me. I would just gloss over and smile faintly. The sad thing was that many of these comments came from people close to me.

David Biebel makes the point in one of his books that Christians are one of the few groups who shoot their wounded. Telling someone who is experiencing the pain of great loss that God is punishing them for some sin is shooting the wounded. It's not your place to speak for the Almighty. He is plenty capable of relaying His own messages.

Also, I must confess here that I have said, "Call if you need anything." I won't anymore. I call the person to see how I can help.

Don't blame God for someone's pain. Don't hyper-spiritualize it either. When someone we love dies, it hurts. All that "It'll be OK" stuff can come later. When people are in pain, all they

want to know is that you care. If you don't know what to say—
and we often don't—just say, "I'm so sorry for your loss."

Remember: immediately following a loss, grievers are not in
their right minds. They're reeling from the loss and many times
are angry, sad, or hysterical. Sometimes they're all these at the
same time. It's part of the grief process that everyone who experiences loss must go through. Be understanding. You may inno-
cently ask a person how he or she is doing and get a face full of
anger. Just roll with it and understand that it's a temporary state
of mind.

Don't be guilty of using the following clichés.

Everything will be OK. How do you know? And even it is,
things will never be the same.

He's in a better place. While that may be true, all we want is
to have him back.

She's not in pain any more. Oh, sure—make me feel guilty for
wanting her here.

I know just how you feel. You do not. And don't even tell me
right now about your loss.

Call if you need anything. Most people will not call. They
would feel awkward or as if they were imposing.

It was in God's plans to take him. How do you know? Did He
tell you? If so, why didn't He tell me?

It's all for the better. Better for whom? I want my baby back.

Your sin caused this. Did God tell you that? How do you
know? Thanks. That's helpful—guilt on top of pain!

Be glad you have three other healthy children. I'm glad I have
three other children. That's not the point. We wanted this child
too.

God must have needed her in heaven. You have to be kidding.
I need her here.

Aren't you relieved that it's over? Relieved that my mom is dead? What kind of question is that?

Time will heal your wounds. While that may be the truth, it doesn't feel like it now. I feel as if I'll never heal.

You were so lucky to have him for 17 years. There's no such thing as luck, and 17 years are not enough. I wanted to share my whole life with him.

You're young—you can remarry. A very insensitive thing to say to someone who lost a spouse. Even if it is true, now is not the time.

You shouldn't be sad—he is with God now. Don't tell me how I should feel.

He lived a long, full life. So what? It wasn't long enough—I need him.

God is going to use this later to help others. I don't want to help others—I want my loved one back!

This happened to you because . . . You don't really know, so don't even go there.

Lord, please give me strength and wisdom to help that someone in pain. I ask that you give me supernatural ability to see what will help this person, the courage to do it, and the devotion not to avoid the person while he or she is in pain. In the precious name of Jesus I pray. Amen.

8 ⁓ WHEN TRAGEDY STRIKES THE COMMUNITY

He heals the brokenhearted and binds up their wounds.
—Ps. 147:3

When the loved one who goes home is elderly or has been ill for a time, the loss is significant, though not a surprise. In the event that multiple deaths occur unexpectedly and to the young, such as the Columbine shootings or tragic car accidents, many more lives are affected. While all grief is numbing and unbelievable, the magnitude of many deaths at once is completely overwhelming and paralyzing.

Micah was four years old the sunny day he and I were in Clement Park, next to Columbine High School in Littleton, Colorado, when the shooting began. We heard the automatic weapon fire from across the grass. By the time we had made our way home, I had an e-mail from our church prayer chain noting that nine kids from our church were still missing. Later, all nine were found physically safe, but the church across the street from ours lost multiple children. Our whole community was in shock and grieving. We needed something to draw folks together. Several area churches had candlelight and memorial prayer gatherings. Folks started making ribbons and pins for the community—especially for the high school students to wear. A couple of kids directly involved wrote and recorded a song with the help of their youth pastor, and area radio stations played it. You can hear it at <http://www.youtube.com/watch?v=hqbo0f9qvxg>.

Several memorials appeared, especially in Clement Park, where people could place pictures, flowers, stuffed animals, and written sentiments. Finding a way to express grief is important, and photographs of the lost ones became priceless.

At the end of spring break a few years ago, a family from our community was on their way home through Wyoming on I-80 in whiteout conditions from a ground blizzard. The resulting 22-car pileup killed six people, four from our community. The mother and three teenaged children were killed in a split second between two semi trucks. Curtis, their father, wasn't with them. He's the sole survivor of his immediate family. Our two oldest boys played basketball with Cameron, the youngest son. My husband was the coach, and Curtis was one of the assistant coaches.

Less than a year after Papa's homegoing, my kids were looking death in the face again. Our boys and all the children and parents of our community were torn to shreds emotionally. Everyone wanted to do something to show how much they cared. Our wonderful neighbor Sheryl brought over ribbons for our boys to wear. After they wore them to school the first day, the boys had scores of orders—everyone seemed to want one. We once again got out the ribbons, glue guns, and needle and thread. We made dozens for friends, teachers, bus drivers, and anyone else who wanted to mark the loss of their friends. Making ribbons didn't take any of the pain away, but it gave our children something to do to show they cared.

Sheryl also made leatherbound books to take to the high school and middle school for all to sign to present to Curtis and the extended family left behind. The inscription on the inside of the books read something like this:

In Memory of Cameron
To Curtis
and the family
From the faculty, students and families
of
West Jefferson Middle School.
With profound sympathy.

The books had 250 blank, lined pages, and we passed it around to the basketball team before giving it to the school to pass around. There were banners, posters, and picture collages of teams and friends. Cameron's basketball team sent a basket of plants to the service in their home state and asked the florist to make sure that after the service it went to the grandmother, who had the gruesome task of identifying the bodies of her daughter and three grandchildren. The wonderful florist in their home-town went to the store and purchased a small basketball to put in the arrangement. During the service, the basketball hopped out of the basket of plants and bounced on the floor. The boys from the team in attendance said they were certain that Cameron had flicked it out to let them know he was OK.

Cameron and his family had not lived in our area that long, but their impact was staggering. The thought of losing our whole family in a split second was more than most of us could get our heads around, let alone our hearts. When a murder, accident, or suicide happens and there are more questions than answers, where do we turn?

I asked a friend from my Bible study whose son had died unexpectedly at the age of 29 what was helpful during that time. She pondered my question and then replied, "Nothing—except the prayers." She said she could feel the love and concern and peace that came through the prayers of those who love and care about her. She remembered that for the first year she was in a complete fog. I wonder if that fog is perhaps our way of not spontaneously combusting when the unthinkable happens. I still don't know why things like Columbine or car accidents or unexpected illnesses steal the ones we love away from us. All I can offer is the assurance that if we'll let Him, in time He will heal us from our brokenness.

This is my prayer for you today if you're in that dark place of despair and pain:

> *Lord, help. I lift up your child to you and ask that you give the peace that passes understanding. Please come into the pain and heal the brokenness. Please walk through this painful time and give us the strength to turn to you for all our needs. Show us that you're there, that you care, and please see us through. In Jesus' precious name I pray. Amen.*

The Lord comforts his people and will have compassion on his afflicted ones.
—Isa. 49:13

Our 14-year-old son asked me why death keeps following us. In our old neighborhood is Columbine High School. Then a friend's son was killed in a car accident. Soon afterward, his beloved principal, who was only in his 30s and the father of five-year-old triplets, and Martin's second-grade teacher both died of cancer the same week. A few months later his grandfather died. Not even a year later, Curtis's family died in a split second. The next year in our new neighborhood came the Bailey school shooting. My boys have been to more funerals than most kids their ages, I suspect.

Indeed, to a young man wracked with grief for the seventh time in as many years, it might seem that tragedy and death are following us. As I sat pondering his question, it occurred to me that death isn't chasing us—it's everywhere. Everyone this side

If you or someone you love loses an infant, please be aware of an organization called the Now I Lay Me Down to Sleep Foundation, found at <http://www.nowilaymedowntosleep.org/start.php>, that will send volunteer professional photographers to take pictures of the deceased baby so the family will have one. They can take photographs of as early as a 23-week-old fetus. The family testimonies on the organization's web site are amazing. Having a photograph to memorialize a lost baby has meant so much to many families.

of heaven dies, some younger, some older, but we all meet the same end. I mused that if we moved to Australia or Outer Mongolia, someone we love would die there too. It happens.

Our goal must then be to live every day as if it matters—and it does, of course. Every person we love must hear it from us often. We're called to spread the good news that there's a remedy to the string of death: eternal life with Christ, and it's free for the asking when we come to Him in repentance.

From the Web site: "The Now I Lay Me Down to Sleep Foundation gently provides a helping hand and a healing heart. For families overcome by grief and pain, the idea of photographing their baby may not immediately occur to them. Offering gentle and beautiful photography services in a compassionate and sensitive manner is the heart of this organization. The soft, gentle heirloom photographs of these beautiful babies are an important part of the healing process. They allow families to honor and cherish their babies and share the spirits of their lives."

Many wouldn't think to take photos but eventually wish that they had.

Lord, please help us to trust your heart. Help us to remember that you have everything under control, that nothing surprises you. Even though we may be in pain and walking through a valley so deep it feels bottomless, you're able to see us through. In Jesus' name I pray. Amen.

9 ～ HELPING CHILDREN DEAL WITH LOSS

Trust in the LORD with all your heart, And lean not
on your own understanding; In all your ways acknowledge Him,
And He shall direct your paths.
—Prov. 3:5-6, NKJV

The most important thing to do for children who are dealing with a loss is to include them in the process. According to The Dougy Center, The National Center for Grieving Children & Families, the one thing kids say they want most is "the truth, the whole truth, and nothing but the truth, told as soon as possible from someone they love and trust in a familiar place."

Children are no different than the rest of us. I interviewed several people who told me they are still mad at their families for not telling them the truth, and especially for not letting them go to the funeral of someone who meant a lot to them. Many of them, adults now, are still harboring an angry grudge against their parents for shutting them out to protect them.

There's no easy time or way to tell a child that someone he or she loved has died. But just like many of the other difficult things that surround death, it must be done, and as soon as humanly possible.

Even if the death is the result of murder or suicide or drug overdose, children must be told. They'll find out sooner or later—usually sooner, when someone at school spills the beans or they overhear an adult talking about it. If you lie to the child about the cause of death, you lose your credibility. As an elementary school teacher, I've seen it happen. Kids can be cruel. Equip them to handle what may be said to them rather than throwing them to the wolves unprepared and unknowing.

If you've already lied, go to them and tell them the truth. Tell them you didn't want them to hurt but that you know they need to know and have a right to know what happened. They'll forgive you, and it might be a great time of healing. Trust is the key factor in every relationship we have, even—maybe especially—with our children. It broke my heart to tell the boys that their Papa had gone home. It felt as though my heart were being torn from my chest cavity, but I had to do it, and so do you. Once they're told, then they can choose what's right for them to do in terms of the funeral.

The key thing to do for children in such situations is to give them choices. Let them decide if they want to go to the funeral. Let them choose if they need to see the body of the deceased. Let them be involved in the funeral if they want to. If they decide they want to take part, let them decide what their involvement will be.

A Pediatrician's Suggestions for Helping a Child Deal with Grief

Below are suggestions from pediatrician Jean Stewart, my dear friend and my son's godmother.

Keep the child's routine intact as much as possible. This includes bedtime, naps, and meals. The familiar is comforting to children and assures them that their lives will go on. Expect children to test the boundaries. Provide gentle comfort, but don't allow them to call the shots. Now more than ever they need the boundaries to be maintained. Sometimes, though, if they're misbehaving, they may need hugs instead of a time-out.

Don't try to hide your own sadness. Let your children see that you're grieving. Tell them you're sad but that you—and they—will be OK. Don't tell them that everything will be the same, especially if one of their parents has died, but tell them, "We'll be OK—we're a family."

Choose your words carefully. Don't say the deceased person went to sleep or that God took him or her. Better wording might be "It was Daddy's time to leave the earth." They might be afraid to go to sleep if you use it to describe death. If you can honestly say the loved went to heaven, say so. If you don't know that the person had a relationship with Christ, don't lie to the children.

Keep age in mind. First, never force a child to view an open casket. Allow school-age children the option. They'll make the decision that's right for them.

Ask a friend in advance if he or she would be willing to take your child or children out to play or take a walk during the funeral if necessary. This will allow you to concentrate on the service if it turns out that the children won't sit quietly. Arrange child care for infants; don't even try to take them to the service.

Watch your children at play. Children will often act out their feelings, fears, and concerns in their play.

Allow your child to sleep with you, but only for a time. If your child wants to sleep with you following the death of one of his or her parents, allow it for a time if you're comfortable with it. Understand that your child is having trouble separating from you at bedtime because he or she is afraid you'll leave too. Try to wean the child back to the family's normal sleeping patterns very soon. Alternatively, you could let him or her sleep on a pallet next to your bed. Be careful not to encourage sleeping with you for *your* need of comfort.

Recognize that sometimes a child will want to go with the deceased parent. Reassure children that their job is to stay here and do the best job they can for God until it's their time to go to heaven. If they're old enough, explain to them that the deceased person's spirit is no longer with the body.

If school-age children or teenagers begin to give away possessions, express a desire to hurt or kill themselves, or talk about joining the deceased person, seek professional help immediately.

Realize that children four years of age and younger don't understand that death is permanent. They'll continue to look for and ask for the dead parent, grandparent, or friend. Gently remind them that the person is not coming back. You may have to say it many, many times, but small children learn by repetition, so be patient as they think of 100 different ways to ask for their lost loved one.

Know that a five-year-old is beginning to understand the finality of death. As children mature, they may need to grieve again as their understanding of death matures. When dealing with loss, children may develop unrelated fears of the dark or strangers or bugs—of anything— and sometimes a school-age or teen child might become obsessive about washing his or her hands or checking to make sure that the door is locked. Seek professional help if you feel overwhelmed in dealing with this phase or if it seems to last a long time.

Recognize the fact that children, like adults, grieve in different ways. Children may appear to be ignoring the whole situation at times. Don't be surprised by this. Allow them time to process their grief when they're ready. However, make sure they don't blame themselves for the death. Elementary school-age children and younger children sometimes believe they have magical thinking and that their thoughts caused this to happen. If nothing they did caused the death, reassure them that it is not their fault.

Again, check out the suggested reading for children in the Resources section of this book.

Teenagers

Teenagers view death in much the same way as adults. The death of a parent or other important person the teenager needs can be devastating, and their faith can be a big help. It's important that they have the chance to talk with adults who are also grieving. Expect teenagers to say things that are difficult. Be open to the possibility that they feel anger toward you or the one who died. Give them plenty of opportunity to talk about their feelings and have them accepted.

Behaviors That Signal the Need for Professional Help

- The child withdraws for more than a week or two.
- The child doesn't seem to care about school or other activities that were important before the death.
- The child has trouble sleeping, does not eat, or starts exhibiting behavior problems such as destroying things.
- The child talks about suicide or makes statement such as "I wish I were dead."

When my father-in-law died, our kids were very upset that they didn't get to say good-bye to Papa. They had planned to go to the hospital the next day to visit him and didn't go the night before. Our oldest son was 14, and I was worried about him. We had just moved and were between churches, so I called a local church and asked if my son could see one of their counselors. He went for only one visit, and it seemed to help him immensely. Sometimes just verbalizing a burden helps get it off your chest.

Lord, I lift up those reading this and ask you to give them your heart on how to help their children deal with the loss they're facing. Give them your words of comfort and healing. In the name of Jesus I pray. Amen.

The Loss of a Beloved Pet

I by no means imply that the loss of a pet can be compared to the loss of a human. I include it because for many—especially children—losing a pet may be a child's first experience with death.

Though I walk in the midst of trouble, You will revive me; You will stretch out Your hand Against the wrath of my enemies, And Your right hand will save me.

—Ps. 138:7, NKJV

Also, the elderly sometimes become completely dependent upon the companionship of a treasured pet in their day-to-day lives, and the loss of that pet can be devastating.

Experts agree that when grief can be expressed, the time needed to recover is often reduced. My friend Cindy said that the death of their dog was very difficult for her son. She framed a collection of photographs of the pooch and bought a stuffed animal that looked similar to their beloved pet. They reminisced about the good times with their dog. That simple remedy gave him much comfort.

If you know your pet is getting on in years, you might prepare your child ahead of time by saying that the pet is nearing the time to go to heaven. Take pictures. Cut a lock of the pet's fur to have as a keepsake. Press a plaster cast of the pet's footprint. Having something tangible to keep as a memento can be very important and comforting to a child. Don't lie to your child. If the pet has died, say so.

Here are a few suggestions for celebrating the life of your pet.

1. Hang a framed photograph of the pet with your family somewhere prominent.
2. Write a story, song, or poem about the pet.
3. Plant flowers or a tree in memory of the pet.
4. Make a donation to an animal rescue organization in your area.
5. Write a letter to the pet.
6. Have a memorial service complete with a eulogy.
7. Buy dog food or kitty litter and donate it to your local animal shelter.

Getting Another Pet

Making the decision to get another pet and when to do it is a personal decision. For our family, we didn't even want to think about it for several months after our dog died. Then Santa Claus showed up with a puppy.

Be careful to let some time pass so that your children don't get the idea that their pet could be easily replaced.

When my mother-in-law's precious pooch died, we waited quite a while before my husband offered to drive her out to see some pups "just to look and see if there are any good ones." They came home with Annie.

Lord, please lead hurting children of yours to a source of comfort. Give them ways to connect with your perspective on the trials they now face, and restore them to joy in your perfect timing. Reassure them that your love never fails. In the precious name of Jesus we pray. Amen.

⌒ RESOURCES

Do not fear, for I am with you; do not be dismayed,
for I am your God. I will strengthen you and help you;
I will uphold you with my righteous right hand.
—Isa. 41:10

A Decembered Grief, by Harold Ivan Smith.

This book is a great resource and encouragement for people dealing with the difficulties of the holiday season (Thanksgiving, Christmas, and New Year's) following the death of a loved one.

A Grief Observed, by C. S. Lewis

Written after his wife's tragic death as a way of surviving the "mad midnight moment," *A Grief Observed* is C. S. Lewis's honest reflection on the fundamental issues of life, death, and faith in the midst of loss.

A Labor of Love: How to Write a Eulogy, by Garry Schaeffer

A Time to Mourn, a Time to Dance, by Margaret Metzgar

Help for the losses in life.

Comforting Those Who Grieve: A Guide for Helping Others, by Doug Manning

An excellent resource for helping others. A must-read for pastors. Great ideas for the night before the funeral.

Dealing Creatively with Death, by Earnest Morgan

Chapter 3 on bereavement and chapter 5 on simple burial and cremation are packed with good information. This book has sold 275,000 copies.

Devotions for the Brokenhearted, by Robin Prince Monroe

This amazing book helped me immensely. If your pain is fresh, and even if it isn't, this is a must-read for anyone experiencing the pain of a loss.

Everybody Wants to Go to Heaven, but Nobody Wants to Die, by David Crowder with Mike Hogan

In an honest, profound look at the connection between death, the soul, and bluegrass music—that's right, bluegrass music—musician David Crowder comes to terms with a Savior who understands suffering and a God who grieves. From exploring the death of the soul in mainstream culture to uncovering slave spirituals in the DNA of bluegrass, Crowder discovers that grief is one of the truest ways to follow Jesus—and realizes that death is not the ultimate calamity.

Final Celebrations: A Guide for Personal and Family Funeral Planning, by Kathleen Sublette and Martin Flagg

This book gives dozens of examples of funerals with songs and ideas for customizing your life celebration. It has an excellent idea for conducting a funeral service for children whose father has died. Useful index in back of book.

Finding Your Way After the Suicide of Someone You Love, by David B. Biebel and Susanne L. Foster

Real help for times of real pain. Offers hope to the hopeless.

For Such a Time as This: A Book of Comfort, by Lanair G. Williams.

A walk through the grief process. Lots of helpful verses and readings and encouragement for the road ahead. Very encouraging.

For These Tough Times, by Max Lucado

When unspeakable tragedies and incomprehensible losses occur, we're sad, angry, even vengeful. And we're full of questions. Why would God allow this atrocity? How can God bring good from such sadness? How should I pray in this time of great suffering? This book includes a search for answers and a request for God's peace and understanding.

For Those Who Hurt, by Chuck Swindoll

Who knows the heartache of having a home split apart? What about someone who understands the loss of a child, the misery of a teenager on drugs, a failure in school, or the loss of a business? God knows you're hurting and wants to be your Comforter. My Aunt Joan suggested this one; she said it made my Uncle Manuel, who couldn't show emotions, cry. She has given it to several in a time of loss.

Funeral and Memorial Service Readings, Poems and Tributes, edited by Rachel R. Baum

This book has entries from poets as diverse as Kipling and Wordsworth to Amelia Earhart and Carl Sandburg. It has selections for every loss. Check it out just for reading. It's good.

Getting Through the Tough Stuff, by Chuck Swindoll

This book with accompanying workbook offers help and hope. Based on Chuck Swindoll's characteristic insight, humor, and powerful yet gentle teaching style, it delivers a strong message of encouragement, hope, faith, and the freedom we have in Jesus Christ. This practical resource will help you to get through the difficult times of life.

Good Grief, by Granger E. Westberg

A simple explanation of the grief process and some helpful ways to work through grief from any loss.

Grace for Tough Times, by Mary J. Nelson

God is with you in the fire! Written by someone who has been through the fire herself, this book takes you on a rare journey into the heart of God. The compelling honesty and wisdom in each devotion will bring renewed hope, no matter what you may be feeling.

Grief Share, by The Church Initiative

A journey from mourning to joy.

Grief—Work It, Let It Be, by S. Leo Richardson

Heaven for Kids, by Randy Alcorn
They'll ask. Be ready. A great resource for parents, arming you with biblical answers to the questions kids ask about heaven.

How to Help a Heartbroken Friend, by David B. Biebel
Written by someone who has been there. He is candid, honest, and helpful. All the books by Biebel have been vastly helpful to me. I heartily recommend them all.

How to Write and Deliver a Loving Eulogy, by Leo Seguin
There aren't many greater honors that can be bestowed upon a person than being requested to provide a summation and reflection of another person's life. It's an honor reserved for the closest and most respected of friends. The book includes sample questionnaires to aid with information-gathering, and it includes five actual eulogies you can use to get firsthand ideas. You'll find many tips about public speaking included, as well as a chapter specifically designed to help you put enthusiasm and real-life fervor into your talk.

If God Is So Good, Why Do I Hurt So Bad? by David B. Biebel
This is his finest book on grief. Honest and candid, Biebel hits the nail on the head. A must-read for anyone struggling through a loss.

If the Dragon Wins, Build Another Castle, by M. Katharyn Meyers
The ABCs of grief. Meyers wrote this book to help her cope with the loss of her son and a brother. It was awarded a Gold Medal in 1999 from The Colorado Independent Publishers Association. Written in ABC format, with each letter of the alphabet dealing with a particular aspect of grief.

Jonathan, You Left Too Soon, by David B. Biebel
David Biebel's first-person account of his struggles to reconcile the conflict between his son's death and God's love is a moving documentary of human loss and divine grace. If you're struggling with the loss

of a child, this is imperative reading for you. To order this book you can e-mail Dr. Biebel at Dbbv1@aol.com.

May I Walk You Home? by Melody Rossi

An excellent resource for anyone wanting to help a loved one in his or her last days. It gives wonderful encouragement for sharing Christ's love with the dying.

My Deepest Sympathies: Meaningful Sentiments for Condolence Notes and Conversations, Plus a Guide to Eulogies, by Florence Isaacs

On Grief and Grieving, by Elisabeth Kubler-Ross and David Kessler

Finding the meaning of grief through the five stages of loss. She is a great author who also wrote *On Death and Dying.*

Planning Memorial Celebrations: A Sourcebook, by Rob Baker

Provides some good examples of memorial services. Great song ideas.

Remembrances and Celebrations: A Book of Eulogies, Elegies, Letters, and Epitaphs, edited by Jill Werman Harris

Restore My Soul, by Lorraine Peterson

A grief companion.

Set Your House in Order, by Crown Financial Ministries

A workbook to organize your finances and plan your estate.

Silent Pain, by Kathy Olsen

When what you know about God's compassion doesn't match how you feel—this book will help you experience the comfort and deeper wholeness that comes from opening your innermost feelings and pain to the One who knows and cherishes you as none other.

Surprised by Suffering, by R. C. Sproul

Contrary to common views that suffering and injustice are a result of sins, which is not necessarily false, or the free will of man goes rampant beyond God's control, whose jargon is called open theism, Sproul affirms the biblical view of the absolute sovereignty of God, who has purposes—good, pleasing, holy purposes for His children in His design, not humanity's design, of every event that happens in their lives, including suffering.

Thank You for Coming to Say Good-bye: Involving Children in Funeral Services, by Janice L. Roberts and Joy Johnson

Has a section for parents, teachers, and church leaders. Gives good insight into what a child understands. Emphasizes how important it is to include children in the process.

The Art of Helping: What to Say and Do When Someone Is Hurting, by Lauren Littauer Briggs

This gem contains "what hurt and what helped" sections for every imaginable loss, plus practical suggestions on what to do for a hurting loved one.

The Book of Eulogies: A Collection of Memorial Tributes, Poetry, Essays, and Letters of Condolence, edited by Phyllis Theroux

The High Cost of Dying: A Guide to Funeral Planning, by Gregory W. Young

An excellent buyer-beware book written by a retired funeral director. Great insights into the industry with lots of helpful information. Great tips to prevent being taken advantage of by funeral directors.

The Needs of the Dying, by David Kessler

A guide for bringing hope, comfort, and love to life's final chapter.

The View from the Hearse, by Joseph Bayly

The author has lost three sons and offers insight on how to deal with death, mourning, and the mourners.

Thoughts for the Holidays: Finding Permission to Grieve, by Doug Manning

You were doing fine—and then here come the holidays. Practical suggestions for surviving the holidays while you're grieving. An excellent resource.

Waiting for Morning, by Cindy Crosby

Hearing God's voice in the darkness.

What About the Kids? Understanding Their Needs in Funeral Planning and Services, by The Dougy Center

The Dougy Center is an excellent resource for getting insights into what children need and want when a loss occurs. Candid and informative. Go to their Web site for a complete listing of their services. See the site address in the "Helpful Web Sites" section

Where Is God When It Hurts? by Philip Yancey

Helps us understand the mystery of pain, why we suffer, and how to cope as well as how to help those we love cope. Yancey is one of my husband's favorite authors. His books are real.

Books to Read to the Kids

Help Me Say Good-bye, by Janis Silverman

Art therapy for children grieving the loss of a loved one. Good for small children. Helpful list of suggestions for kids.

Sarah's Grandma Goes to Heaven, by Maribeth Boelts

Another beautifully illustrated book. It's a great story and even tells about the funeral. A great one for elementary school-aged kids and younger too. Great section in the back for parents.

The Day Scooter Died, by Kathleen Long Bostrom

Great story book for a child who has lost a pet. Especially good because the boy in the story feels guilty that he may have caused the death. Lots of issues dealt with in this one. Good for elementary school-aged children and younger. Great section in the back for parents.

The Fall of Freddy the Leaf, by Leo Buscaglia

I loved this book when I was teaching school. It shows that everything dies and the delicate balance between life and death.

The Tenth Good Thing About Barney, by Judith Viorst

This is a classic book about the loss of a pet. It might be good to read following any loss. Viorst also wrote two other books I should note here: *Alexander and the Terrible, Horrible, No Good, Very Bad Day* is one of my favorite kid's books. She has another one out about loss that I haven't read yet but might be worth looking into called *Necessary Losses.* It's an adult book.

Tiger Eyes, by Judy Blume

A boy journeys through grief after his father is shot. For ages 10 and up. Judy Blume is an excellent author.

What About Heaven? by Kathleen Long Bostrom

This book answers many questions for little kids. It is part of the Little Blessings Series. Preschool- and kindergarten-aged kids would like it.

What Happens When We Die? by Carolyn Nystrom

Good for school-aged children as well as younger ones. Answers lots of questions in a story format. Shows scripture reference for each idea.

What Is Heaven Like? by Beverly Lewis

Beautifully illustrated by Pamela Querin. This is the book to read if your child says he or she wants to go to heaven to be with the one who died. It's a good story about a boy who lost his grandpa and is on a mission to find out what heaven is like.

When Dinosaurs Die: A Guide to Understanding Death, by Laurie Kransny Brown and Marc Brown

This book addresses children's questions and fears head on. It gives good suggestions for things to do after a funeral to help with grieving the death of a loved one. Gives examples of different beliefs about death.

～ WEB SITES

For cremations
<http://funeraldepot.com/Funeralandcremationnetwork.htm>

For posting an obituary in the newspaper
<www.legacy.com>

To hear the Columbine Memorial Song: "Friend of Mine"
<http://www.youtube.com/watch?v=qbo)f9qvxg>

To find a place that releases pigeons, butterflies, or ladybugs
<www.abutterflyrelease.com>
<www.butterflyreleasecompany.com>
<http://www.naturescontrol.com/ladybugs.html>

National Funeral Directors Association Web site for current
trends
<http://www.nfda.org/page.php?pID=78>

To help you plan
<http://www.funeralplan.com>

Help for children who are grieving
<www.dougy.org>

To remove the names of deceased individuals from marketing
lists
<https://www.ims-dm.com/cgi/ddnc.php>

To create an online memorial
<http://www.remembered-forever.org>

Information about becoming a organ donor
<www.donor-awareness.org>

For a pet memorial
<http://www.4everinmyheart.com/?gclid=CP671qf30ZACFSG8godt2E
TXA>

Rainbow Bridge pet loss web site
<http://www.petloss.com>

Pet loss poem list for your burial service
<http://www.petloss.com/poems/poems.htm>

Sample service for a pet
<http://www.in-memory-of-pets.com/christianservice.php>

Pet sympathy gifts
<http://www.gifts.com/interests/pets-animals/ohra224icp10n?sid
=google:CNT_PETS_members.fortunecity.com:P>

Pet sympathy cards
<http://rainbowsbridge.com/Rainbow_Boutique/Rainbow_items/card
s.htm>

Pet memorial. Will make a hardbound or electronic memorial
of your pet

∿ GLOSSARY OF TERMS ASSOCIATED WITH DEATH AND DYING

Administrator: Any court-appointed person or body put in charge of the estate of a person who passed away with no valid will.

Autopsy: A careful medical study to find the cause of death.

Beneficiary: Any person who receives the proceeds of an insurance policy or will.

Bequest: A gift of property received from a will.

Bereaved: The immediate family of the deceased. May include close friends.

Casket: Same as coffin. Burial box for a dead person.

Casket liner: A container to surround the casket in a grave.

Codicil: An amendment to a will that either modifies or revokes part of it.

Columbarium: A building designed for the housing of urns of cremated remains, in niches.

Contest: A legal challenge to a will.

Corpse: A dead body.

Cremation: The incineration of a corpse until only calcified bone fragments are left.

Cremains: The calcified bone fragment remains of a cremated body crushed into indistinguishable bits.

Crypt: An underground room or vault, often below a church building, used as a burial chamber or chapel or for storing religious artifacts.

Death certificate: an official, legal document signed by a doctor or coroner certifying the death of an individual and stating cause of death if known. The death certificate is required to settle an estate and arrange for the internment and many other legal issues pertaining to death.

Disposition: The manner in which the remains of a deceased individual will be disposed of (such as ground burial or cremation and ash-scattering).

Embalming: A procedure that replaces the blood in a deceased person with formaldehyde to temporarily preserve the body. Embalming is not required in any state or by any federal law.

Epitaph: The inscription on a tombstone or monument commemorating the person buried there.

Eulogy: A spoken or written tribute to a person who has died, usually given at a funeral or memorial service.

Escheat: The state takes over the estate when there are no beneficiaries or heirs.

Estate tax: Federal and state taxes applied to property transferred by death.

Executor/Executrix: Male or female named as the person who administers an estate.

Funeral: A service created to honor the memory of a dead person, usually shortly after the death, often with the body or cremains present. The funeral is designed to minister to the family members and friends of the deceased and is often the beginning of the healing process from the loss.

Funeral director: The professional who maintains the funeral home, prepares the body for burial, and oversees burial and other services.

Headstone: The marker for the grave of the departed. Gives names, dates of birth and death, and sometimes an epitaph.

Hearse: A special vehicle for carrying the casket.

Internment: Burying of a dead body in a grave.

Intestate: Leaving no legally valid will.

Living trust: A trust that was established during the life of the trustee.

Living will: A legally binding document relaying the wishes of an individual about his or her medical care, especially concerning resuscitation and life-sustaining technology.

Mausoleum: A large tomb for housing a body above ground, especially one that is ornately decorated and/or made of expensive stone.

Memorial service: A service much like a funeral but that can be held at any time after the death and often does not have the body or cremains present. The purpose is to help the grieving begin the healing process.

Mourn: To feel or express sadness or grief for a death or other loss.

Mortuary: A licensed, regulated business that provides for the care, planning, and preparation of human remains after a death.

Niche: A compartment in a columbarium that houses an urn with cremains in it.

Next of kin: Closest living relative.

Obituary: Announcement of a death, especially in a newspaper, often with a short biography and dates and times of services.

Organ and tissue donation: The giving-away of parts of a dead person's body that may save a living person.

Perpetual care burial plot: A burial plot that is mowed and weeded and kept up.

Perpetual care trust funds: A portion of the cost of a burial plot that is set aside in a trust fund for its ongoing care (such as grounds-keeping and mowing).

Probate: The legal certification of the validity of a will.

Register book: A blank book for guests at a visitation and funeral service to sign. Some have space for leaving a message to the survivors.

Right of survivorship: When a joint property owner provides for the passing of all property into the hands of the surviving joint owner. This will erase the need for probate.

Service folder: A handout given at the beginning of a funeral service that designates the order of the service. It often has a photograph of the deceased, his or her obituary, a favorite verse, and other information pertaining to the deceased and the day's events.

Survivors: Those left when someone dies. Usually refers to immediate family or close friends; may be those who are named in the will.

Testator: A person (especially a man) who has made a legally valid will.

Tomb: A grave or other place for burying a dead person.

Trust: Usually a fund but may consist of other property held and managed by one person for the benefit of another (or others).

Urn: A container made for holding cremated remains.

Vigil: In Roman Catholicism, a service held on the eve of the funeral service.

Visitation: A scheduled time when an embalmed body is on display, usually held at a funeral home.

Widow: Wife of a person who died.

Widower: Husband of a person who died.

Will: A legal document that states what a person wishes to be done with his or her belongings and property after death. It may also include directions on what the person prefers be done with his or her body and other things.

⌒ FORMS TO GET ORGANIZED

Personal Wishes for Funeral Service or Memorial Service, or Plans by Loved Ones for the Service

Date _____

Full name of deceased _____

Social Security number _____

Veteran? No _____ Yes _____

Branch of service _____

For Veterans—discharge papers are stored _____

Papers necessary for insurance and financial records are stored

_____

Address at time of death:

_____

_____

_____

Occupations _____

Favorite hobbies and activities _____

_____

Date and place of birth _____

Father's name and place of birth _____

_____

Mother's maiden name and place of birth _____

_____

Spouse's name _____

Spouse surviving? _____

Date and place of marriage _____

_____

Children's name(s) and current residences

_____

_____

_____

_____

_____

_____

Grandchildren's names

_____

_____

_____

_____

_____

_____

_____

_____

_____

_____

_____

_____

_____

_____

Great-grandchildren's names

Great-great grandchildren's names

Disposition of the Body

_____ Burial in a casket

Type of casket

_____ Pine box

_____ Hardwood box

_____ Metal box

Cemetery preference name _____

_____

Address _____

_____

_____

Lot number if already owned _____

Papers for the lot are stored _____

_____ Bury in mausoleum

_____ Cremation

_____ Bring cremains home in an urn or container provided by family

Container for the cremains to be _____

_____ Give cremains to _____

_____Bury the cremains with a headstone

_____Bury in a niche in a crypt that houses many deceased

_____Cremains buried in half-grave spot

_____Church houses cremains

Church name, address, and phone number _____

_____

_____ Spread cremains

Location _____

_____ Donate body to _____

Medical College for research

Papers for this arrangement are stored _____

Contact _____

_____ Organ and tissue donor

Contact number _____

Papers for this arrangement are stored _____

_____ Embalm

_____For closed casket service—not necessary

_____For service, then cremate

_____For viewing at a service or to ship body

_____Do *not* embalm

The Service

Newspaper notice and/or obituary: Yes _____ No _____

In which newspaper(s) _____

_____

_____

Already written? No _____ Yes _____

Stored _____

Memorial service at _____

(church or facility)

Scripture selections

_____

_____

_____

_____

Desired speaker(s) or pastor(s)

_____

_____

_____

_____

Song choices

_____

_____

_____

_____

Vocalists and songs to be sung

_____

_____

_____

_____

Congregational hymns

_____

_____

_____

Memorial, foundation, or charity to which family and friends
may contribute _____

_____

Send the flowers to _____

_____

Favorite flowers include _____

_____

Veterans organization to participate: _____

_____

Suggested pallbearers: _____

_____

_____

_____

_____

_____

_____

Honorary pallbearers _____

_____

_____

_____

_____

_____

_____

Graveside service: Yes _____ No _____

Before the funeral or after _____

Refreshments after the service: Yes _____ No _____

Types _____

_____

_____

_____

Provided by _____

_____

_____

Other requests or comments _____

_____

_____

_____

_____

_____

Signed _____ Date _____

Witnesses (optional)

_____ Date _____

_____ Date _____

_____ Date _____

_____ Date _____

⌒ BIBLE VERSES

Cast all your anxiety on him because he cares for you.

—1 Pet. 5:7

We are always confident, knowing that while we are at home in the body we are absent from the Lord. For we walk by faith, not by sight.　　　　　　　　　—2 Cor. 5:6-7, NKJV

He will swallow up death forever! The Sovereign Lord will wipe away all tears.　　　　　　　　　—Isa. 25:8, NLT

Let not your heart be troubled; you believe in God, believe also in Me. In My Father's house are many mansions; if it were not so, I would have told you. I go to prepare a place for you. And if I go and prepare a place for you, I will come again and receive you to Myself; that where I am, there you may be also.

—John 14:1-3, NKJV

By the sweat of your brow you will eat your food until you return to the ground, since from it you were taken; for dust you are and to dust you will return.　　　　　　—Gen. 3:19

He will wipe every tear from their eyes. There will be no more death or mourning or crying or pain, for the old order of things has passed away.　　　　　　　　　—Rev. 21:4

We know that when this earthly tent we live in is taken down—when we die and leave these bodies—we will have a home in heaven, an eternal body made for us by God himself and not by human hands. We grow weary in our present bodies, and we long for the day when we will put on our heavenly bodies like new clothing. For we will not be spirits without bodies.

—2 Cor. 5:1-3, NLT

I am convinced that neither death nor life, neither angels nor demons, neither the present nor the future, nor any powers, neither height nor depth, nor anything else in all creation, will be able to separate us from the love of God that is in Christ Jesus our Lord.   —Rom. 8:38-39

Blessed are those who mourn, for they will be comforted.
                                                    —Matt. 5:4

Blessed are the peacemakers, for they will be called sons of God.
                                                    —Matt. 5:9

If any of you lacks wisdom, he should ask God, who gives generously to all without finding fault, and it will be given to him.
                                                    —James 1:5

Now is your time of grief, but I will see you again and you will rejoice, and no one will take away your joy.   —John 16:22

May the God of hope fill you with all joy and peace as you trust in him, so that you may overflow with hope by the power of the Holy Spirit.   —Rom. 15:13

Then my head will be exalted above the enemies who surround me; at his tabernacle will I sacrifice with shouts of joy; I will sing and make music to the Lord.   —Ps. 27:6

Let us run with endurance the race that is set before us, looking unto Jesus, the author and finisher of our faith.
                                                    —Heb. 12:1-2, NKJV

The Lord comforts His people and will have compassion on his afflicted ones.   —Isa. 49:13

My children, we should love people not only with words and talk, but by our actions and true caring.   —1 John 3:18, NCV

As I was with Moses, so I will be with you; I will never leave you nor forsake you. —Josh. 1:5

I am with you always, to the very end of the age. —Matt: 28:20

Trust in the Lord with all your heart, And lean not on your own understanding; In all your ways acknowledge Him, And He shall direct your paths. —Prov. 3:5-6, NKJV

Be still, and know that I am God. —Ps. 46:10

I can do all things through Christ who strengthens me. —Phil. 4:13, NKJV

He heals the brokenhearted and binds up their wounds. —Ps. 147:3

God has breathed life into all Scripture. It is useful for teaching us what is true. —2 Tim. 3:16, NIRV

Though I walk in the midst of trouble, You will revive me; You will stretch out Your hand Against the wrath of my enemies, And Your right hand will save me. —Ps. 138:7, NKJV

In that day the wolf and the lamb will live together; the leopard and the goat will be at peace. Calves and yearlings will be safe among lions. . . . The cattle will graze among bears. Cubs and calves will lie down together. And lions will eat grass as the livestock do. —Isa. 11:6-7, NLT

Do not fear, for I am with you; do not be dismayed, for I am your God. I will strengthen you and help you; I will uphold you with my righteous right hand. —Isa. 41:10

comfort and support for a grieving heart

Holidays are difficult to face when you're grieving. Days of celebration are now marred by unpredictable emotions and an intensified sense of loss.

This compassionate book offers illustrations, insights, and words of comfort to help lessen the pain and heartache you expect to feel during the holidays. With keen perception, understanding, and empathy, author and grief-counselor Harold Ivan Smith helps you acknowledge your grief and learn to let God transform the season into a time of grace and healing.

A Decembered Grief
Living with Loss While Others are Celebrating
ISBN: 978-0-8341-1819-5

comfort, connection, and hope

for parents who have lost a child

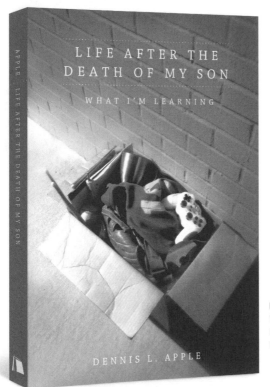

Life After the Death of My Son
What I'm Learning
Dennis L. Apple
ISBN: 978-0-8341-2365-6

In *Life After the Death of My Son,* Dennis Apple explores the unspeakable pain, helplessness, and frustration he and his wife have experienced since the sudden death of their teenaged son. Using excerpts from his journal, Dennis shares his painful yet promising story and offers honest understanding and gentle guidance to those walking similar paths.

BEACON HILL PRESS
OF KANSAS CITY

Available wherever books are sold.